INTRODUCTION

SPEAKING OF HIS PAINTING, the American artist Arthur Dove said, "We cannot express the light in nature because we have not the sun. We can only express the light we have in ourselves." It is not by accident that we have invented imagery that ovecomes the limitations of language. Common to all of us is the manipulation of truth that we call poetic license.

Our lives are filled with every conceivable ploy to escape the ordinary. We embellish the simplest events of our mundane lives. These "tall tales" are efforts to describe the remarkable interaction of imagination and something even more quixotic—that which many of us innocently call "the truth." Clearly tall tales are not true, and yet, even for those who fervently believe in something as obsolescent and undependable as Truth, such stories are not counterfeit.

The universal inclination to produce a reality that is truer than the one before us—even the everyday creation of tall tales—is simply the most commonplace aspect of a profound disposition of the human psyche: the making of myths. In his book *Myths To Live By*, Joseph Campbell tells us that "it is a curious characteristic of our unformed species that we live and model our lives through acts of make-believe." We are myth makers. We are legenders. Of all the animals we alone are capable of dreaming ourselves into existence.

This book is about those dreams and myths and the countless ingenious ways in which we ritualize them as both social and personal experiences. In this new edition I have given particular emphasis to the interaction between group and individual myth. This concern for personal myths and their dynamic interface with the myths of the community is especially important in our time when society is no longer supported by a truly pervasive and significant system of beliefs. It is a time when the creative impulse has been internalized and has few sources in the external world. It attests to the fact that even our mythologies must be dynamic if they and—through them—we are to survive. The most ancient tales and rites are no more valid than those of our day. The power of the dream is still in the capacity for dreaming.

The process by which this complex network of myth and ritual makes itself visible and effective is metaphoric, poetic, imaginal. At its simplest it is the telling of tall tales. At its most profound it is the creation of masterworks of art.

RITUAL
OF THE WIND

Sun Dance encampment with the dance arbor showing the center pole and Thunderbird's Nest, right, and the ceremonial lodge of the Women's Matoki Society, left. Probably northern Blackfoot, in Alberta, Canada.

NORTH AMERICAN INDIAN CEREMONIES, MUSIC, AND DANCE

Ritual of the Wind

JAMAKE HIGHWATER

Front Cover: Gan Dancers
   Painting by Rance Hood.
   Courtesy Tribal Art Gallery,
   Oklahoma City, Ok.

Editorial Director: Robert Walter
Editor: Martha Cameron
Book Design: Jos. Trautwein/Bentwood Studio

Revised edition © 1984 Methuen Publications, Toronto.

Library of Congress Cataloging in Publication Data:

Highwater, Jamake.
   Ritual of the wind.

   Bibliography: p.
   Includes index.
      1. Indians of North America—Rites and ceremonies.
2. Indians of North America—Religion and mythology.
3. Indians of North America—Dances. 4. Indians of North
America—Music. I. Title.
E98.R3H7 1984   394 ·   83-80563

ISBN 0-912383-02-X

Printed and bound by:
   Royal Smeets Offset B.V.
   The Netherlands

for RICHARD THURN

It was the wind that gave them life.
It is the wind that comes out of our mouths now
that gives us life. When this ceases to blow we die.
In the skin of our fingers we can see the trail of the wind;
it shows us where the wind blew when
our ancestors were created.

WASHINGTON MATTHEWS
Navajo Legends, 1897

The best-known rite of the modern Seminoles is the Green Corn Dance, a series of dances and ceremonies lasting four to six days. Depicted here is a circle dance. The first day is given over to the preparation of the dance circle and sweat baths taken by the holy man and his assistants. Wood is gathered for a "dance fire," and afterward a ball game is played between the young men and women. The fire is lighted and several dances are performed. The second day is devoted to feasts held in the big house, at which only the men participate. On this day a white heron is killed and its feathers are collected for use in the ceremony.

At midnight the men begin to fast. Early on the third day the medicine bundles are brought out and a black drink is prepared and consumed by the men. The Feather Dance is staged twice in the morning and twice in the afternoon. At night the contents of the medicine bundles are displayed. At dawn on the fourth day, the holy man hides the sacred bundles and then ritually scratches the men and boys, using a small implement in which needles have been inserted. The long fast is broken, and for the first time, the Seminoles eat the new corn crop. For them a new year has begun.

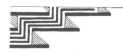

CONTENTS

In the past humans invoked gods to cause the unpredictable, and viewed the world as a temperamental place, full of caprice and random occurrences. Then, with the growth of science, nature came to be regarded as lawful and the universe to be organized according to strict mathematical principles. Now, with the threat of a naked singularity (in physics), we are brought back once more to the chaos of the early days—to a universe in which anything at all can happen.

PAUL DAVIES
The Edge of Infinity

Rituals which resound with great antiquity are found among the Tewa Indians of New Mexico. In the Corn Dance (also known as the Tablita Dance) the men dress in white kilts over which is tied a tasseled rain sash. A fox skin is tied to the back of the belt as a reminder of humanity's kinship with animals when all beings had tails. Behind the right knee is a turtle shell with deer-hoof tinklers that resound as the dancers move. A gourd rattle that is held in the right hand makes the sound of falling rain. Skunk fur over the moccasins protects against evil. A bandoleer over the left shoulder is decorated with conus shells from the distant Pacific Ocean, trade objects of great value. A cluster of parrot feathers is worn on top of the head, while jewelry and sprigs of evergreen are used to complete the traditional costume of the Corn Dance. The women dancing just behind the men wear the black manta tied at the waist with a red and green sash; they are barefoot, and carry evergreen boughs in both hands. On their heads they wear tablitas, thin wooden plaques cut in terraced patterns like rainclouds and painted with star and sun symbols. The woman's manta is typically worn off the left shoulder. (Santa Clara Pueblo, New Mexico, 1911)

At approximately the same time that the sedentary, agricultural Tewa Indians of Santa Clara Pueblo were performing fertility rites to coax a bountiful harvest from the earth, the hunting-warring Flathead Indians of western Montana performed a victory dance known as the Grass Dance, because the performers traditionally wore a grass bustle knotted under their waist sash, a symbol of the grassy plains of the battlefield. The Grass Dance has mistakenly become known as the War Dance—presumably performed before battle—whereas it was actually a dance of victory that probably originated among the Omaha Indians (and is therefore also called the Omaha Dance). The grass bustle and headdress—made of deer tail and known as a roach—gradually evolved into the very bright and lavish costume of the Fancy Dance of modern Plains Indians.

The costume and the steps of the Fancy Dance grew out of exuberant victory rites; but to survive the turn-of-the-century censorship of white missionaries and government officials and also because of the inherent dynamics of all cultures, the dance substituted its political and religious intentions with fanciful purposes, becoming a spectacular and rather garish exhibition of individual performing prowess and elaborate regalia.

The costumes and paraphernalia of rituals are grounded in the ceremonial life and material culture of various Indian tribes. Such rites and costumes make a people's cosmology visible and dramatic. Just as the brilliant feathered bustle of the Fancy Dance had its origin in a bustle of grass, the highly complex masks and carved house posts of the North West Coastal Kwakiutl Indians are grounded in the relationship of the tribe to the cosmos and the relationship of the individual to the group. This is a Kwakiutl Cannibal Ceremony. Squatting, long-billed masked dancers represent huge, mythical birds of the Winter Dance cycle: Kotsius and Hohhuq, servitors in the house of the man-eating monster Pahpaqala-nohsiwi, who is honored with this highly theatrical dance. The mandibles of these dramatic wooden masks are controlled by strings, permitting the dancers to transform themselves from an outer being to an inner cosmic power. (1910)

The cosmic and the ethnic merge in rituals; the emotional life of the tribe is ritualized in relationship to its special environment. The White Deerskin Dance of the Hupa Indians of northern California is unique in costume and ceremonial forms because it perfectly captures the relationship of a people to their special world.

Thus it creates a ritualistic "language," which is understood by every initiated member of the group and which therefore provides each tribal person with a positive relationship to the group.

In their most rarified and imaginative forms, these rituals transcend ethnicity and become remarkable metaphors of the relationship between the ceremonial life of a people and the universality of human experience. Here members of the Qagyuhl tribe dance to save the life of the moon during an eclipse. To these people of the north an eclipse results when a sky creature tries to swallow the moon. The people dance around a smoldering fire of old clothing and hair. The stench rises into the realm of the devouring creature and causes him to sneeze and then to disgorge the threatened moon. (1910)

Cowichan, masked dancer of the Coastal Salish people. (1912)

PRELUDE
On the Trail of the Wind

P RIVACY HAS A highly mystic and deeply significant value to Indians. Whites often misunderstand the reluctance of many Indians to reveal and therefore to debilitate their personal identity. This sacred view of the self is seen as a peculiar form of secrecy. Information which has almost no meaning to white people is the crux of a realm of the self for some Indians, who are sometimes embarrassed and often amused by the personal questions ethnologists and tourists ask them: their age, where they were born, the names of their relatives, their social position, income, marital status, and so forth.

For decades many Indians haven't told ethnologists the truth, as only in this way could they retain the power of their privacy. For most Indians honesty is a matter of telling someone truly how they feel and what they think. It doesn't have anything to do with personal information.

There is tribal as well as personal privacy, a fact that helps to explain the secrecy of clans, societies, and holy people. The power of certain songs, actions, rites, and paraphernalia is endangered by the aggression of hostile strangers. To what extent secrecy dates from pre-Columbian times and how much of it resulted from later censorship and Christian missionary morality is hard to say. Even in the highly conservative Southwest, where ritual life has changed only slightly in five or six centuries, we know that early army officers and missionaries were permitted access to the underground sacred chambers called kivas, to burial grounds and ritual events. Whenever the tribal edict of secrecy evolved, one thing is certain: its violation was till very recently punishable by exile, dispossession, and even death. However, some Indians are willing to cooperate with outsiders as "informants."

A secret can be so well kept that even when it is told you can't make any sense of it. One day in New Mexico I was taken by five Pueblo friends to the basement of a museum where several portfolios had been stored, with the agreement between curators and tribal leaders that the secret pictorial works would not be made public for fifty years or more. My Indian friends opened these folios for me. I quickly searched through the old, yellowed sheets of paper on which self-taught artists had used pencils and crayons to draw secret rites. I could see absolutely nothing worthy of secrecy. I continued studying the drawings, but I could not grasp any reason whatever for their being so carefully guarded from strangers.

Perhaps my experience was a bit like that of whites who have made investigations to uncover some bit of private information about an Indian, only to discover that the "truth" reveals nothing very impressive or important. For white people a secret usually hides something devious or precious; for an Indian a secret is important not because of what it hides but because privacy itself is a valuable possession.

The privacy of Indians is an individuating as well as a unifying aspect of their culture. It is preserved because it is essential to the framework of personality among Indians—as individuals and as tribes.

The peyote cult has become the central rite of the Native American Church, an intertribal religion that came from Mexico in the late nineteenth century, and that combines many principles of Christianity with an ancient peyote ritual. Members assemble in the mescal tepee at about 8 in the evening. The peyote chief sits against the west wall, facing east, with the drummer on his right and the cedarman on his left. The fire tender sits near the entrance. The chief distributes ritual items such as a water drum, fan, rattle, and

An earthen altar in the shape of the crescent moon is used to hold peyote buds. During the songs and prayers peyote buds are passed to each person, chewed, offered to the altar, and then swallowed. The peyote induces visions, which are the primary purpose of the ceremony. Meetings are held for reasons of health, birthdays, thanksgiving, or Christian holidays such as Christmas and Easter. Participants sit in the tepee during the entire night. The rites end at dawn when water and breakfast are brought into the tepee. (1892)

1
THE INITIATION

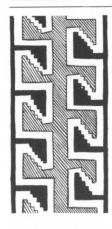

In the House Made of Dawn

IT IS A COLD NIGHT at Window Rock, tribal center of the huge Navajo reservation in Arizona. We sit on beautiful rugs, huddling as close as possible to the fire in the center of the room. Instead of the traditional hogan of logs and sod, the house in which we sit is a spiritless little rectangle of cinder block, and instead of the traditional fireplace there is simply a large oil drum on an earthen hearth with a doorway cut in the side into which we place bits and pieces of bark and branch we have collected from the edges of the endless asphalt highway that runs rampant through Navajo-land. Like the ancient fireplace of the traditional Navajo home, this improvised oil drum is in the center of the room; a large stovepipe fitted to the top of the drum disappears through the plasterboard ceiling. The house is ugly, but the fire is good, crackling nicely as we sing and talk.

We put our mugs of coffee on this stove to keep them hot. Sitting on the floor in the unfurnished room, we feel very happy tonight. Patú, a maker of Navajo jewelry, has presented me with a handsome turquoise ring, and I repeatedly hold my hand up to the firelight and nod to him and his wife while I admire the large, shiny stone. We are connected to a marvelous sense of ourselves, and it is good to be together. But our visitor seems uncomfortable. He looks into the only other room of the little house of my friend Patú. Two little boys lie across the bed, asleep. They dream of turquoise and silver, rabbits and Superman and John Wayne.

The white man will not sit down; he needs to search for a chair. But there are no chairs in this modest house. So he stands in the corner where the woman is making fried bread in an electric frying pan. There is no stove or sink. Water is fetched in a ten-gallon plastic container from the gas station four miles down the road. A small refrigerator keeps the meager food supply fresh.

Patú's wife Magga brushes back her thick black hair and glances feebly at the white guest. "We are looking for a better house," she murmurs apologetically, "but they are difficult to find."

In the bedroom one of the boys coughs, and Magga hurries to him when he awakens and whimpers. "No wonder he's sick," the white man says, glancing with undisguised dismay at the broken glass in the room's only window. "What these children need is a good doctor."

Suddenly our song ends and we are ashamed, for the guest has made us feel self-conscious. When he leaves us he will talk of the Navajo world as if he knew and understood it. No matter how much our guest believes he grasps Indian values and appreciates differences, he will nonetheless judge Indians by his own standards—

In the Navajo Initiation Ceremony, performed when boys come of age, the divinities, or yei, are represented by impersonators. Shown here are Talking Power and Fringe Mouth. (1905)

which he irreversibly believes are superior to all others. When he leaves he will talk of "poverty" and "squalor." He will not speak of our song or my beautiful new ring or the mystique that binds us. He will not understand our contentment with a dirt floor that is warm in winter and cool in summer. He will probably pity my Navajo friends without intending any offense. And because he cannot believe anyone can be happy without the things essential to his own life, he will say that what Indians really need are cinder-block houses with all the modern conveniences.

There is a difference between tradition and squalor. But to see the difference we must undergo a cultural initiation and transcend the ethnocentricity that confines us to a single tradition—for the greatest distance between people is not space but culture. The initiation requires the stranger not only to know what another people knows but also to feel what they feel. The initiation teaches us that it is not necessary to be the same as everyone else in order to be equal. On that cold night in Arizona what Patú and his people needed more than pity or tolerance was the right to retain their special relationship to their own world of realities—a world as immense as any other, a world of strong rain and strong wind and ceremonial salvation.

The prayer for rain is the prayer for salvation of the spiritual body. Wind is the precursor of the rain, but before the ceremonial performers can become the rain they must first become the wind. The great prayer that follows is the dramatic climax of the Navajo Night Chant, and it represents for Patú and his people a source of power and meaning far greater than anything yet offered to the Navajo by Western civilization.

The prayer is addressed to the thunderbird of pollen and is carried into the wind-swollen sky that is the house of storms:

> *Tsegihi!*
> *House made of the dawn.*
> *House made of evening light.*
> . . . .
> *Dark cloud is at the door.*
> . . . .
> *The zigzag lightning stands high up on it.*
> *Male divinity!*
> *Your offering I make.*

In this fusion of dance, song, and music is "art" before art exists. Prior to 1492 there is no equivalent in North American Indian languages of the West's self-conscious idea of art. The purpose of the Night Chant is curiously practical from the Western standpoint, despite the fact that it abounds in subtle expressiveness. Though it possesses an important relevance to the whole life-style and matrix of the Navajo world, the Night Chant is not the utterance of a disembodied lost soul suffering the torments of original sin and damnation. It is, instead, a highly physical event concerned with a practical reality, specifically a curative ceremony enacted by a holy man ("doctor") to remedy the ills of a tribesman ("patient"). But in the use of the word "patient" (which is generally applied to the person who sponsors the ceremony) the significance of the illness from the Indian viewpoint is entirely lost. For the "disease" to be cured is an ailment of the spiritual body which has mysteriously lost touch with the universe. The idea that spirituality can be associated with the body is extremely remote from the Western belief in the dichotomy of mind and body, spirit and flesh. It was until very recently inconceivable in the world of Christianity and Judaism that there could be any relationship between spiritual and physical reality.

To many white people dancing is a form of mindless amusement. Not until the turn of the century was dance used as an art form by people like Isadora Duncan and Martha Graham. Until then body movement possessed a very humble and static existence in Western civilization. It was so detested by both the church and the synagogue that it was officially prohibited after a brief but important expressive use in early religious ceremonies. It is difficult after centuries of belief in the mortification of the flesh (and the celebration of the disembodied soul) for most white people to grasp the possibility of a "spiritual body" in which spirit and flesh are unified. The Indian concept of harmony among all things is so alien to the West that many whites cannot conceive of a spiritual conviction that can be communicated through dance—

unique expressive act in which, more than any other, there is immediacy and a perfect unity of thought and feeling. As Indians have often stated to the bewilderment of whites, dancing is the "breath-of-life" made visible. This concept of the breath-of-life is discovered everywhere in the unique spiritual world of Indians: in the ceremonial stem of the sacred pipe, in the heart line of animals imprinted on pottery, in the rite of inhaling the first light of day, and the conferring of blessings by exhaling. All these symbolic images and gestures are associated with the wind and with the breathing of the universe—the visible motion of the power that invests everything in existence.

When ethnologist Washington Matthews was collecting histories and legends among the Navajos in the 1890s, he was told something by a holy man that made a deep impression. "It is the wind that gave them life," the old one whispered, the "them" referring to First Man and First Woman, the Navajo Adam and Eve, to whom the wind imparted the breath-of-life. "It is the wind that comes out of our mouths now that gives us life," the holy man continued as he gestured to his chest and throat. "When this ceases to blow we die." Then he held his wrinkled hand to the light of a lamp and gazed at his fingertips. "In the skin of our fingers we see the trail of the wind," and he then made a circular motion to indicate the whirlwind that left its imprint in the whorls at the tips of the human finger. "It shows us where the wind blew when our ancestors were created."

*   *   *

When we envision the dawn of human society, we generally see a time when humanity was awed by the mysteriousness of the world. When confronted by lightning or fire, by birth or death, we imagine that the emotions and thoughts of primordial people were welded into a compulsive gesticulation of the body and by the soft intonation of fear, wonderment, or grief—much as we still witness involuntary movement and utterance among people in extreme states of emotion. It is generally presumed by specialists in cultural history that these primal motions of the human body ultimately became dance while the murmurs became incantation and song. As the dance evolved and the songs became more complex, people could not sing and dance simultaneously, and so the day came when some people stood aside to make music while others remained in the dance circle, where they could devote all their energy and concentration to the enchantment of their dance. Though separated by reason of expediency, music and dance continued for centuries wedded to each other and to the first moment in human history when expressivity was born of responsiveness.

The music developed in North America by Indians is one of the world's distinctive musical idioms, for no other people have produced duplicate sounds even when they created similar instruments, such as drums and rattles and whistles.

The most obvious aspect of Indian music is the prevalence of drums and rattles and the characteristic harshness of vocal reproduction—a sort of flat, unemotional sound which has certain parallels in vocal music of the Near East. Indian music is essentially unison vocal composition with percussive accompaniment. Voice production is typically strong in accent, with tension in the vocal organs and an Eastern pulsation on the long notes. It is music of a linear structure, in some ways not unlike the music of Asia. It does not excel in harmonic development. The melodic structure descends predominantly from higher to lower pitch in either terraced or downward-

An elaborate studio portrait of a
young Yuma musician with his flute.

Apache and his unique fiddle, photo-
graphed in a studio about 1882.

cascading intervals. Melodic polyphony—the simultaneous voicing of two or more
melodic lines—is nonexistent, except for an occasional drone-type accompaniment
of a voice or voices using a single, sustained pitch, or the tradition by which women
often sing in unison with the men but an octave higher. Instruments are used strictly
for rhythmic accompaniment; there is very little purely instrumental music, such as
solo drumming or any other kind of instrumental virtuosity as we know it in Western
music. Structurally, uneven bar lengths and asymmetrical rhythmic patterns are far
more common than consistent measure lengths.

Besides the already mentioned percussive instruments, some tribes used wooden
flutes, mostly for the music of courtship. And in the case of the Apache there is also
a very basic stringed instrument called an Apache fiddle that is bowed and plucked.
In recent years there has been a revival of flute carving and playing among several
tribes, even those that do not have a known history of flute music. The people of the
Dakotas were excellent flutists and carved handsome instruments out of cedar and
tied them with skin thongs. The Yaqui play Pacura flutes, and the Papago and Pima
have their own style of wind instruments.

The songs of Indians are related to various central activities. There are, for instance, songs of healing which arise from the mystery of life and death. Numerous ceremonies are cycles of curative songs concerned with restoring personal health as well as sustaining the fertility of crops and the abundance of game. There are also individual songs that are highly personal insofar as they came out of lonely suffering and trauma:

> *It is only crying about myself*
> *That comes to me in song.* [Nootka]

Personal songs are also the embodiment of an acquired vision with great power for its owner. Apart from the curing songs, which usually possess fertility overtones, there are also songs exclusively concerned with growth and abundance, addressed to elements of nature and filled with marvelously keen observation:

> *Blue evening falls,*
> *Blue evening falls,*
> *Near by, in every direction.*
> *It sets the corn tassels trembling.* [Papago]

The Indian world has a deep reverence for solitude and silence. Children are taught at a very early age to sit still and enjoy their solitude in the belief that from this quietude come the most elevated of creative experiences. From this solitude come songs of a special, highly personal nature evolved out of the secret self. Such songs are not shared but are kept strictly to one's self. Dream songs are highly prized by Indians and, like songs of vision, come only to those who search for them. Fasting, long vigils, and sometimes the use of drugs such as jimsonweed are used to bring the song-bestowing dreams. Among the Plains tribes such songs are highly personal and highly valued as property, while among the Pueblo people a dream is likely to present a potter with new designs for the whole community. There are also songs of death, similar to those of the Japanese. The brave song—or death song—is a steadfast and eloquent expression of a man who grasps the fact of his own death. It is sung only at times of utter desolation or when the singer stands in the face of death. Other death songs are composed spontaneously at the very moment of death and are chanted with the last breath of the dying man.

> *The odor of death,*
> *I discern the odor of death*
> *In front of my body.* [Dakota]

Every moment of life and death is celebrated by Indians in songs and in rituals. There is no aspect of the world that is not worthy of astonishment.

Music, like all the arts, is built upon the viewpoint of a culture, and the music of Indians has almost nothing in common with the attitudes that give substance and character to the music of the white world. The Indian viewpoint contrasts with the Western attitude in many ways. First of all, most Indians have a more or less Eastern view of things. Fundamentally it is expressed in an attitude of synthesis—in other words, thinking in terms of a gestalt or whole, whereas most white people are concerned with analysis—thinking not of the whole but of the parts in a more or less scientific fashion.

Indians view the natural world as perfect. Therefore they are quite content with their situation and attempt to live harmoniously with it rather than to alter and dominate it. They are not inclined to make vast judgments that would place some things in a position of superiority to others. In the Indian world the fox is a brother with a spirit of his own. Another Indian trait is the favoring of subtlety and poetic understatement. To Indians the white people seem to exaggerate everything, to emphasize specific details without any grasp of the whole. But because of their holistic attitude, Indians tend to derive meaning from context, while white people think in terms of separate entities with separate meanings and values.

With these differences in mind, it is a bit easier to grasp the nature of American Indian music. For one thing most Indians regard music as an element of a much larger activity—as part of the life process—and not as a separate aesthetic entity. Music is the breath-of-life, an organic process rather than an end product. It is generally thought that Indian music is functional, that it is used as part of other, nonmusical activities of daily life. But this is simply the result of an analytical, non-Indian way of looking at music. To the Indian, music and dancing are indistinguishable from worship, which is itself indistinguishable from living.

Because of the inclination to understate, most Indian music and dancing is reminiscent of Japanese haiku and painting, where symbols have been minimized and meaning is conveyed through metaphor. Song texts contain entirely or partly meaningless syllables. Texts may also include archaic words, loanwords, or even special phonemic alterations. These devices make song texts very different from the spoken prose of a tribe and tend to obscure the meaning of songs. The inclination of non-Indians is to view such restricted use of lyrics as primitive, whereas Indians consider this procedure an important device of civilized restraint and poetic suggestiveness.

Music is highly valued for its magical powers. If the music is well performed it is "good spirit" rather than "beautiful," an aesthetic term that seems highly superficial and artificial from the Indian point of view.

Despite long exposure to the variety and complexity of European music, Indians are still inclined to preserve the methods and values of their own music, using at most voices, drums, rattles, flutes, and a simple form of fiddle. To the European this is backward, but Indians cannot conceive of improving that which is already perfect. They have never had to ask themselves the burning mid-twentieth-century question, How much progress is enough progress? They have never believed in progress as a value unto itself.

2
THE CEREMONY

Navajo dancers led by the divinity Talking Power, at the annual Fourth of July Powwow in Flagstaff, Arizona.

I Bring the Whirlwind That You May Know Each Other

AT THE TRADING POST and airport of Oljato, Utah, you will find two antique gas pumps, a masonry ruin, a couple of one-prop air taxis in the midst of a sprawling red desert, and a few clouds of dust. The summer day buzzes with flies and then suddenly lapses into an immense silence. Occasionally a green mule-drawn wagon rumbles past, or perhaps a pickup truck, bent and battered into one of those quintessential wrecks in which Indians chug through their precious wilderness. Edward D. and Virginia W. Smith run the trading post, the oldest business in the area. Their screen door bangs every now and again as a Navajo man, his hair tied in a queue and his head topped by a black Indian-Joe hat, comes in for his mail and perhaps a plug of tobacco, while his wife, in a long skirt and a blanket, sits in the wagon with the kids bobbing around her like corks in a pond. You can grab your camera and, if you are fast, snap a picture. They will not care, but they will surely turn their heads away shyly and become intensely silent. If you offer them a dollar, the kids will scramble down and take it. They might feel a little better, and perhaps they will smile the next time you take their picture. They are too innocent to understand that they are a terminal people. And that makes them unbearably tragic.

Their mother, however, will gaze away with nobility, ferocious in her silence. She will collect her children, and she will avoid her husband's eyes as he lumbers back to the wagon. He ignores your remarks as if you did not exist, and he lifts his massive physique into the driver's seat, leaving you alone in a silence filled with dust and disdain.

You will probably feel a mixture of embarrassment and pity as you watch them go. You will also be annoyed that you came such a long way to see the real life of Indians who don't particularly want to show it to you. When you ask where various ceremonies will be held, Indians change the subject. And when you happen upon a dance, you do not feel especially welcome. You are baffled. Is it possible that such highly intriguing events are not performed for audiences? And if the rituals are not public performances, then what are they?

No one answers you.

Is it possible that Indians don't care whether people understand them or not? Yes, it is possible.

Is it possible that Indians scorn and reject the compassion of whites who want them to become equal members of a great society? Yes, it is possible. Indians do not consider themselves a "minority." They see themselves as the only natural products of the ancient land newly named America. Many Indians are not anxious to have their fair share of the spoils of the United States of America. They don't long for acceptance by the dominant culture. Some Indians want to remain separate—so much so that their essential activities and beliefs are kept secret.

Elsewhere, as you travel through the America of Indians, you may not encounter resistance or secrecy or hostility. In tourist towns where people make a living by turning Indian life into a show, you can get lessons in the War Dance (which isn't a war dance) much as you can learn Lovely Hula Hands from another subjugated native people. There is no question of it; the world of assimilated Indians will be much easier. But such a world will also be a questionable comfort—a forest without tigers. The Indians will be more defenseless than friendly. They will sell you Indian jewelry that they have converted from fakes made in Hong Kong. But among the Mountain Utes you will get no welcome whatever. They will turn from you like deer frightened by a rifle shot. And in Oklahoma you may spend hours talking unknowingly to Indians while you are looking for them.

The Indian is as various as any large array of people on Earth. It is as difficult to generalize about Indians as it is about Europeans. Both groups represent not one but numerous cultures. But one thing is certain: Indians were isolated from the rest of humanity until 1492, when invaders who came from the sea might just as well have come from another planet, so staggering were the differences between them and the great race they found in what is now called North and South America. There is abundant evidence that Indians greeted the strangers with hospitality. We are all aware of how the explorers, conquistadores, and missionaries greeted the Indians. The contempt of Indians is their response to several centuries of contemptuous white behavior. Until 1924 Indians were not U.S. citizens, and until 1934 it was officially unacceptable for Indians to be instructed in any aspect of their heritage: languages, arts, religions, or life-styles.

Is it any wonder that the most valued aspects of Indian life were hidden from missionaries and legislators who saw Indian culture as a threatening and tenacious symbol of savagery? While American colonial towns were collecting imported European culture, the native people of America were carefully sustaining what they could of their own heritage. It was not easy. By the 1920s the vast Indian population of North America had been depleted by genocide, neglect, and disease, as well as by religious and legislative persecution. Only 200,000 Indians survived. In some areas whole tribes had vanished. In other parts of the country two or three old people recalled their native languages—of more than 200 distinct languages once spoken in North America alone. Among many of the Indian nations pottery, painting, and basketmaking, ritual, dance, songs, and ceremonies had almost vanished.

But they did not vanish. There was a tenacity in the survivors that helped them recreate their Indian world from the frail germinal memory of their race—like the place in the acorn that envisions the oak tree. The warriors of the 1890s keenly understood both their military defeat and their possibility of survival through cultural tenacity. The Cheyenne Ghost Dance of 1893 proclaimed:

> *I bring the whirlwind that you may know one another.*
> *We shall live again!*

And indeed they do live again! Under every rock of this enormous continent there is still a trace of the Indian past—a marvelous heritage that emerges like the water of a secret spring out of the depths of the old earth and its ancient people, is carried forward in the pulse of Indian ancestry, and lives within the people like rings of an ancient tree, which meticulously record many summers and countless generations. It comes from the days when the rivers were clear and the prairie was filled with sweet grass, when the giant redwoods were mere saplings in the first frail dawns of California.

In this heritage that was kept alive by Indians there are substances and shadows so rich that they overflow and flood the sadly arid world created by Western civilization. Today there is a sudden awakening of interest in Indians. This advent of a wide public concern for Indian culture comes at a more opportune time than the earlier efforts of a few ethnologists to raise the American consciousness of Indians and the positive examples of their world. This is a time when all over the world there is a deeply felt movement away from technology in daily life, a time when there is a desire to grasp both the nature-orientation and the philosophical otherness of primal peoples who have not been unconditionally shaped by the thrust of Western civilization and all its obvious ills. The exploration of Indian sensibility might be a highly significant source of understanding of the colossal mess in which the industrial world now finds itself. Through the culture produced by Indians in North America an alternative world view is glimpsed—a vision of things that anthropologist Carlos Castaneda has aptly called "a separate reality." Its uniqueness is so remote from the dominant civilization's attitudes that numerous studies, experiments, and debates are now under way as white people try to permeate that fascinating and remote separate reality. People are discovering among Indians a vast alternative mentality, a brilliance of ideas, and a process of life unknown in the West. At the same time people are having difficulty understanding that American Indians—who look to whites so thoroughly savage and uncivilized, who live in what is considered to be squalor and ignorance, and who failed to discover the Industrial Revolution, nuclear weaponry, God, and Jesus—have nonetheless created all the stupendously graceful and lofty culture that fills their lives.

It is a strong lesson in humility for people who have lived for centuries with the idea that there are only two worlds—a civilized one that creates and an uncivilized other that destroys. The world cannot be so simply divided, and the cultural imperialism that has separated the world for far too long cannot survive the evidence at hand.

The appeal of Indians and their persistent culture is no longer based on curiosity and exoticism. Something more fundamental attracts and instructs people in regard to Indians. Despite all the apparent ethnic specialness of Indians, their ideals and ways possess great universality. That potent significance prompts this exploration of the ritual basis of Indian life: ceremonies and dances viewed from the standpoint of the Indian rather than the vantage of alien observers. These ceremonies and dances are fundamental to the whole life process of Indians. All the fragmented intellectual preoccupations of white people are unified for Indians in their rituals. The unknown is translated into human experience, the ineffable made visible. It is a process very similar to the creation and function of art in the societies of the West. In a crucial way the ceremonial life of Indians depicts a more startling and revealing discovery of America than the accidental one that took place in 1492.

The Navajo Night Chant

THE NIGHT CHANT, or Yeibichai, is the cosmic world of the Navajo made visible through ritual.[1] In its most direct context it is a form of therapy conducted by a chanter for the cure of a "patient." However, the Night Chant has a more inclusive position in Navajo life. In the participation of assistant singers, impersonators of divinities, initiates, spectators, and dancers, as well as the use of sand paintings, the Night Chant becomes a panoramic expression of Navajo cosmology.

The ceremony opens at sundown and closes eight and a half days later at sunrise. The first four days are devoted to purification. At midnight on the fourth day the divinities are ceremonially awakened. These powers descend from their homes and appear in the great sand paintings that are made by the chanter (a shaman) on the fifth through the eighth days of the ceremony. These complex iconographic drypaintings manifest the divinities and make it possible for them to touch their bodies to the patient's body and in this manner to transmit their power.

The Night Chant is accompanied by singing and dancing. But like many Indian ceremonies there is more emphasis upon ritual action than dancing as it is understood in the West.

The ceremony takes place in a hogan, a lodge of timber and sod traditional to the Navajo, roughly eight feet high in the center and twenty-five feet in diameter at the base. The curtained doorway faces east. In the center of the ceiling is a smoke hole and beneath it a circular open hearth. The participants of the ceremony are the chanter, who has a complex shamanistic role in the rites; the patient, who normally commissions the ceremony on his own behalf; assistants to the chanter, various singers, relatives, and friends of the patient who are honored by an invitation to attend the non-public parts of the ceremony; and the dancers and holy people who become manifestations (impersonators) of the powers that descend to participate in the rites.

PART ONE: THE PURIFICATION

First Day—Day of the East

AT NIGHTFALL the lodge is consecrated. The chanter enters and moves sunwise (clockwise) around the lodge, rubbing the four supporting timbers with cornmeal. A crier stands at the door, calling, "Come on the trail of song."

The breath-of-life is the first rite of exorcism. Entering with friends and relatives, the patient takes the seat of honor, west of the central fire. Twelve rings of bent sumac have been placed in the basket. Talking Power enters with a collapsible square of peeled willow. He opens the square and places it around the patient's waist, chest, shoulders, and head. Then he withdraws. In a moment a Female Divinity enters and takes one of the sumac rings from the basket and touches it to the patient's vital parts. At the patient's mouth she ravels the yarn used to truss the ring. Then she leaves, dragging the ring behind her. This same action is now repeated by Gray Power, who removes a second ring from the basket. Then a second Female Divinity enters and removes a third ring. Talking Power reappears with the open square, and the entire sequence in which three rings have thus far been unraveled is performed again—and again until all twelve rings have been removed from the basket.

CHANTER

*From a place above, where he stands on
high,*

*Hastsheayuhi, where he stands on high,
says, "Your body is holy," where he
stands on high.*

[1]Excerpt based on John Bierhorst, *Four Classics of Indian Literature*, 1974, used by permission. Additional sources include Edward S. Curtis, *North American Indian*, 1907, and Washington Matthews, *The Night Chant*, 1902.

The chanter and his assistants prepare four sacrificial offerings, and four lengths of reed grass are cut and painted with representation of the divinities destined to receive them.

CHANTER

A little one now is prepared. A little one now
*   is prepared.*
For Hastshehogan, it now is prepared.
A little message now is prepared,
Toward the trail of the he-rain, now is
*   prepared.*
As the rain will hang downward, now is
*   prepared.*
A little one now is prepared. A little one now
*   is prepared.*
For Hastsheyalti, it now is prepared.
A little offering now is prepared,
Toward the trail of the she-rain, now is
*   prepared,*
As the rain will hang downward, now is
*   prepared.*

The painted reeds are filled with native tobacco.

CHANTER

Now the yellow tobacco am I.
Now the broad leaf am I.
Now the blue flower am I.
With a trail to walk on, that am I.

These cigarettes are sealed at each end with moistened pollen and lighted. The chanter applies pollen to the patient's body, making a motion as if bringing it from the sun. He then takes the four offerings and places them in the patient's hands. Now the patient recites after the chanter, line by line:

CHANTER AND PATIENT

Owl!
I have made your sacrifice.
I have prepared a smoke for you.
Today take out your spell for me.
Today I shall recover.
Happily may I walk.
May it be happy before me.
May it be happy behind me.
May it be happy below me.
May it be happy above me.
With it happy all around me, may I walk.
It is finished in beauty.
It is finished in beauty.

The prayer is repeated three times, involving in turn the divinities Hastsheayuhi, Hastsheeltlihi, and Echoing Stone, each of whom is to receive one of the offerings. Now the assistants take the completed offerings outside the lodge and lay them down in the prescribed positions, and in this way give them to the holy ones.

SINGERS

Across the Tsheyi Canyon from the other side
*   he crosses,*
On a slender horizontal string of blue he
*   crosses,*
For his offering of blue, upon the string he
*   crosses.*
Across the Tsheyi Canyon from the other side
*   he crosses,*
On a slender horizontal string of white he
*   crosses,*
For his offering of black, upon the string he
*   crosses.*

At midmorning the assistants construct a small conical sweathouse over a shallow pit. Carrying plumed wands and led by the chanter, who scatters pollen in their path, the participants proceed from the lodge to the sweathouse.

SINGERS

This I walk with, this I walk with.
Now Hastsheyalti I walk with.
These are his white plumes I walk with.
In old age, the beautiful trail, I walk with.
It is I, I walk with.

Separating the wands into male and female groups, the chanter plants them around the sweathouse. Now the patient enters and sits beside the heated stones that provide the steam as water is poured over them. The chanter, outside, mixes the chant lotion and the night medicine.

CHANTER

In the House of the Red Rock
There I enter;
Halfway in, I am come.
The corn plants shake.

Hastsheyalti and a Female Divinity appear, and as the patient comes out of the sweathouse they touch his body with the wands. Then the patient drinks the night medicine and bathes himself in the chant lotion.

The sweathouse is dismantled and the party returns to the lodge. The chanter anoints the patient with pollen and inserts some pollen into the patient's mouth and into his own mouth.

Ina hwie! my grandchild, I have eaten.
Hastshehogan. His food I have eaten.
The pollen of evening. His food I have eaten.
In old age wandering. I have eaten.
On the trail of beauty. I have eaten.
Ina hwie! my grandchild. I have eaten.
    Kolagane!

Now the party withdraws.

Sprinkling dry pigment on the lodge floor, the chanter prepares a small sand painting featuring the four sacred mountains of the Navajo world, and a trail leading into their midst. At the doorway the crier calls: *"Bike hatali haku."* The patient enters, walking slowly along the trail of the painting and going to the mountains. Hastsheyalti follows.

SINGERS

In a holy place with the divinity I walk.
On Tsisnadzhini with the divinity I walk,
In old age wandering with the divinity I walk,
On a trail of beauty with the divinity I walk.

Now the patient reaches the center of the sand painting.

CHANTER

With beauty may I walk.
With beauty before me, may I walk.
With beauty behind me, may I walk.
With beauty above me, may I walk.
With beauty below me, may I walk.
With beauty all around me, may I walk.
In old age wandering on a trail of beauty,
    lively, may I walk.
In old age wandering on a trail of beauty,
    living again, may I walk.
It is finished in beauty.
It is finished in beauty.

Kneeling, Hastsheyalti takes sand from each of the mountains of the sand painting and applies it to the patient's body. The patient kneels as coals are removed from the fire and placed in front of him. Over these coals the chanter sprinkles a powder of feathers and resin. The coals are now extinguished and the sand painting is obliterated. Then the party withdraws.

Second Day — Day of the South

T HE CRIER calls at sunset to begin the second rite of exorcism, the evergreen dress. The patient enters the lodge and is draped with the evergreen dress—garlands of spruce symbolizing the bonds of disease. The twin war divinities, Nayenezgani and Tobadzhistshini, appear.

SINGERS

In a land divine he strides,
Now Nayenezgani strides,
Above on the summits high he strides,
In a land divine he strides.
Now Tobadzhistshini strides,
Below on the lesser hills he strides,
In a land divine he strides.

The divinities move sunwise around the patient, cutting loose the knotted garlands of spruce branches.

SINGERS

The Slayer of the Alien Powers,
That now am I.
The Bearer of the Sun
Arises with me,
Journeys with me,
Goes down with me,
Abides with me,
But sees me not.
The Child of the Water,
That now am I.
The Bearer of the Moon
Arises with me,
Journeys with me,
Goes down with me,
Abides with me,
But sees me not.
I am the Slayer of the Alien Powers.
Wherever I roam,
Before me
Forests are strewn around.
The lightning scatters;
But it is I who have made it.
I am the Child of the Water.
Wherever I roam,
Behind me
White waters are strewn around.
The tempest scatters;
But it is I who have done it.

The divinities withdraw. The chanter places fragments of the evergreen dress over the patient's head. With a grass brush he brushes away the evil and forces it out through the smoke hole in the roof.

CHANTER

The rain descends, the corn grows up.
I sweep it off. I sweep it off.

After the incense is burned the party withdraws.

On the second morning the chanter and his assistants prepare two "long" offerings sacred to the Hastsheyalti and Hastshehogan of a shrine known as the House of Horizontal White. Each of the offerings is a tobacco-filled reed attached to a string which passes through five perforated jewels and is decorated with feathers at the end. The chanter places the offerings in the patient's hands, leading him in a prayer.

CHANTER AND PATIENT

In the House of Horizontal White,
He who rises with the morning light,
He who moves with the morning light;
Oh Hastsheyalti,
I have prepared your sacrifice.
I have made a smoke for you.
His feet restore for him.
His limbs restore for him.
His body restore for him.
His mind restore for him.
His voice restore for him.
Today your spell take out for him.
This very day your spell is taken out.
Away from him you took it.
Far away from him it has been taken.
Far away from him you have done it.
Happily he will recover.
Happily he has recovered.
Happily his interior will become cool.
Happily, feeling cold he may walk around.
It is finished again in beauty.
It is finished again in beauty.
In beauty may you walk, my grandchild.
Thus will it be beautiful.

Each offering is made and then they are taken outside to be sacrificed by placing them in prescribed positions where the divinities may find them. The patient is given incense. The sweatbath ritual is repeated, this time with the sweathouse built to the south of the lodge. Fifty-two offerings are prepared during the afternoon: four tobacco-filled reeds and forty-eight wooden pegs.

Third Day—Day of the West

AT NIGHTFALL the third rite of exorcism begins. The crier calls and the party assembles and enters the lodge. Fifty-two offerings are sacrificed, after which the party withdraws.

The third morning prayer ritual follows the pattern of the second, now with a set of eight offerings sacred to the divinities of the shrine known as the House Made of Dawn. Four of the offerings stand for the Atsalei dancers to be encountered during the ninth night of the ceremony; four nearly identical prayers accompany these offerings.

CHANTER

Tsegihi!
House made of the dawn.
House made of evening light.
House made of the dark cloud.
House made of male rain.
House made of dark mist.
House made of female rain.
House made of pollen.
House made of grasshoppers.
Dark cloud is at the door.
The trail out of it is dark cloud.
The zigzag lightning stands high up on it.
Male divinity!
Your offering I make.
I have prepared a smoke for you.
Restore my feet for me.
Restore my legs for me.
Restore my body for me.
Restore my voice for me.
This very day take out your spell for me.
Your spell remove for me.
You have taken it away for me.
Far off it has gone.
Happily I recover.
Happily my body becomes cool.
Happily I go into life.
My body feeling cold, may I walk.
No longer sore, may I walk.
Impervious to pain, may I walk.
With lively feelings, may I walk.
As it used to be long ago, may I walk.
Happily may I walk.
Happily with abundant dark clouds may I walk.
Happily with abundant showers may I walk.
Happily with abundant plants may I walk.
Happily on a trail of pollen may I walk.
Happily may I walk.
Being as it used to be long ago, may I walk.
May it be beautiful before me.

May it be beautiful behind me.
May it be beautiful below me.
May it be beautiful above me.
May it be beautiful all around me.
In beauty it is finished.
In beauty it is finished.

In the early afternoon the chanter lays pieces of amole in a tightly woven basket, adds water, and gives the mixture to an assistant, who beats it until suds rise. The chanter then sprinkles pollen over the surface of the suds, and the patient is lathered to the accompaniment of the Darkness Songs:

CHANTER

The rain descends, the corn comes up.
It foams, it foams.

The necklace and jewels of both the patient and the chanter are washed. Then the patient is rinsed, and rubbed with cornmeal.

CHANTER

From his body, it is rubbed away.
In old age wandering, it is rubbed away.
On the trail of beauty, it is rubbed away.

Fourth Day—Day of the North

H ASTSHEYALTI, accompanied by Hastshehogan, plants a sapling in the earthen floor of the lodge, bends it toward the patient, and ties it to a mask fitted to the patient's face. When the sapling and mask fly back, the evil influences are pulled away from the patient's head. Now the patient scatters pollen on the masks of the powers which have been laid out on the lodge floor. Barely audible prayers accompany this action. Afterward, pollen bags are passed through the audience of friends and relatives, and anyone who wishes to eat a portion of the pollen may do so.

Women carrying dishes of ceremonial food enter and move sunwise around the fire of the lodge. The masks are now symbolically fed from a bowl of cornmeal mixed with water. At midnight the chanter takes up each mask and "shakes" or awakens it as he sings the Waking Song.

CHANTER

He stirs, he stirs, he stirs, he stirs.
Among the lands of dawning, he stirs, he
  stirs;
The pollen of the dawning, he stirs, he stirs.
Now in old age wandering, he stirs, he stirs.
Now on the trail of beauty, he stirs, he stirs;
He stirs, he stirs, he stirs, he stirs.

In beauty may I dwell.
In beauty may I walk.
In beauty may male kindred dwell.
In beauty may female kindred dwell.
In beauty may it rain on my young men.
In beauty may it rain on my young women.
In beauty may it rain on my chiefs.
In beauty may it rain on us.
In beauty may our corn grow.
In the trail of pollen may it rain.
In beauty before us, may it rain.
In beauty behind us, may it rain.
In beauty below us, may it rain.
In beauty above us, may it rain.
In beauty all around us, may it rain.
In old age,
The beautiful trail.
May I walk.

After the prayer the rest of the night is devoted to the chanting of song cycles, selected by the chanter. The following songs are among the most stately of the song cycles:

CHANTER

The sacred blue corn-seed I am planting.
In one night it will grow and flourish,
In one night the corn increases,
In the garden of the House Power.
The sacred white corn-seed I am planting.
In one day it will grow and ripen,
In one day the corn increases,
In its beauty it increases.
Listen! It approaches!
The voice of the bluebird is heard.
The corn grows up. The waters of the dark
  clouds drop, drop.
The rain descends. The waters from the corn
  leaves drop, drop.
The rain descends. The waters from the plants
  drop, drop.
The corn grows up. The waters of the dark
  mists drop, drop.
Shall I cull this fruit
Of the great corn-plant?
Shall you break it? Shall I break it?
Shall I break it? Shall you break it?
Shall? Shall you?
I pulled it with my hand.
The great corn-plants are scattered around.

I pulled it with my hand.
The standing plants are scattered around.

The singing continues until the crier, shouting from outside the lodge door, announces the first streak of dawn. The songs cease and the chanter prays as the patient withdraws.

The sweathouse is built for the last time to the north of the lodge. Thunder Songs are chanted.

CHANTER

The voice that beautifies the land!
The voice above,
The voice of thunder
Within the dark cloud,
Again and again it sounds,
The voice that beautifies the land.
The voice that beautifies the land!
The voice below,
The voice of the grasshopper
Among the plants,
Again and again it sounds,
The voice that beautifies the land.

PART TWO: THE HEALING

Fifth Day

SHORTLY AFTER nightfall a basket is turned upside down on the floor of the lodge and beaten to the accompaniment of songs. Ushered in by Hastsheyalti and a Female Divinity, the initiates (children) are sprinkled with cornmeal and flagellated with a blade of yucca if male, or, if female, massaged with an ear of corn. The divinities unmask. In turn the initiates try on the mask of the Female Divinity; they sprinkle pollen on the masks, they inhale the incense that has been burned. Then the basket is turned upright.

Sprinkling powdered pigments on the floor of the lodge, the chanter and his assistants prepare the first great sand painting known as the Picture of the Whirling Logs—depicting Hastsheyalti, Hastshehogan, and other powers of succor seated on the arms of a cross (which floats on the surface of a whirlpool), encircled by the ribbonlike figure of the Rainbow Power. When the sand painting is completed, the chanter deposits meal on the sacred figures, plants plumed wands around the outside of

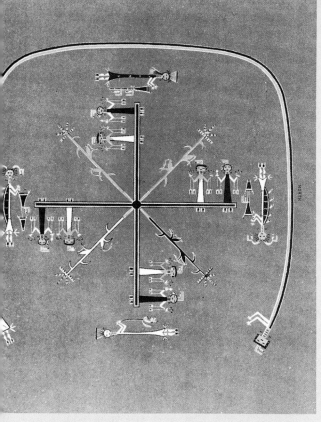

Picture of the Whirling Logs, the first great sand painting. (1902)

the picture, sets a cup of medicine between the hands of the Rainbow Power, and sprinkles pollen. Now a Male Divinity enters, takes the cup, and after offering it symbolically to the pictured powers of the sand painting, he gives it to the patient to drink. Taking dust from the various bodily parts of the divinities of the sand painting, the chanter applies it to the corresponding parts of the patient. Songs of the Whirling Logs accompany the rites.

CHANTER

The great corn arrives.
The child-rain arrives.
In a way of beauty arrives.
Grasshopper arrives.
From the west arrives.
Vegetation arrives.
Pollen arrives.
In a way of beauty arrives.

Now the Male Divinity withdraws. The chanter provides incense and the sand pictures is obliterated.

Sixth Day

AGAIN THE basket is turned down and beaten in acccompaniment to songs. After the songs the basket is turned upright again and the chanter waves toward the smoke hole to drive out the evil influences that were captured and imprisoned beneath the basket by the power of the songs. The chanter

Picture with the Fringe Mouths, the third great sand painting. (1902)

Sand paintings, the best known element of the various curing rites, are used by most tribes of the Southwest. Navajos have evolved sand painting to a complex art, with as many as a thousand separate designs. Here the chanter and two assistants use dry materials of various colors to create a sand painting.

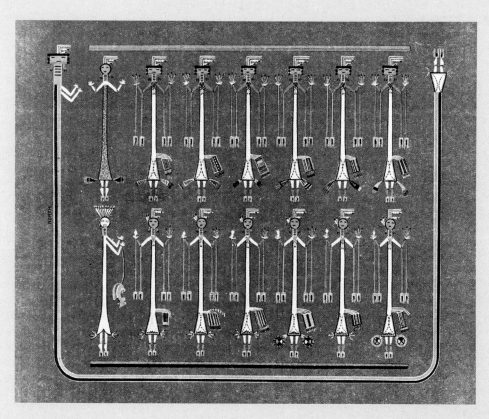

45

and his assistants repeat the previous day's sand painting ritual, producing the second great painting; again the ribbonlike Rainbow surrounds the divinities, this time representing the ninth-night Naakhai dancers.

Seventh Day

ONCE AGAIN the basket is turned down, and after songs are sung it is turned upright as before. The third great sand painting is made; a modified Rainbow encircles the representation of twelve divinities, including those called Fringe Mouths. Turning sunwise, the patient now enters the lodge, approaches the completed sand painting, and submits once again to the ritual whereby the dust from various parts of the bodies of the divinities is touched to the corresponding parts of the patient's body. After each use of the sand paintings they are carefully obliterated.

Eighth Day

A RITE OF SUCCOR is performed. Afterward, inside the lodge, the patient presents offerings to each of the three divinities who take part in the rite. In other nine-day chants of the Navajos a fourth great painting is customarily made on the eighth day of the ceremony. But in the Night Chant, one of the sand paintings is said to have been withheld—or forbidden—by the gods. In its place, Nayénezgani, Tobadzhistshíni, and Hastsheyalti perform a rite of succor similar to that of the preceding day.

The Navajo Night Chant, or Yeibichai, is performed in a space called "the dancing ground," a sanctified clearing. Here, in this dancing ground, several yei perform: Talking Power, Fringe Mouth, and Slayer of the Alien Powers, as well as the Slim First Dancers.

PART THREE: THE REPRISE

Ninth Day

FOUR GREAT FIRES are made on each side of a level space called the dancing ground, just in front of the lodge. Beyond the dancing ground stands a newly constructed arbor. Spectators, sometimes numbering in the hundreds, gather along both sides of the dancing ground. This portion of the ritual is open to strangers.

The chanter's assistants paint with white earth the bodies of the dancers selected to be the four Atsalei, or Thunderbirds. The dancers enter the arbor where they prepare for the Dance of the Thunderbirds. Now, fully costumed and led by Hastsheyalti, the Thunderbirds emerge from the arbor and approach the dancing ground. The crier calls: "Come on the trail of song!" The patient emerges from the lodge and sprinkles the dancers with meal. Addressing the Thunderbirds, the patient recites after the chanter, line by line:

CHANTER AND PATIENT

In Tsegihi,
In the house made of dawn,
In the house made of the evening twilight,
In the house made of dark cloud,
In the house made of the he-rain,
In the house made of the dark mist,
In the house made of the she-rain,
In the house made of pollen,
In the house made of grasshoppers,
Where the dark mist curtains the doorway,
The path to which is on the rainbow,
Where the zigzag lightning stands high on
    top,
Where the he-rain stands high on top,
On, Male Divinity!
With your headdress of dark cloud, come to
    us,
With your mind enveloped in dark cloud,
    come to us!
With these I wish the foam floating on the
    flowing water over the roots of the great
    corn.
I have made your sacrifice.
I have prepared a smoke for you.
Today, take out your spell for me.
Today, take away your spell for me.
Away from me you have taken it.
Far off from me it is taken.
Far off you have done it.

Happily I recover.
Happily for me the spell is taken off.
In beauty I walk.
With beauty before me, I walk.
With beauty behind me, I walk.
With beauty below me, I walk.
With beauty above me, I walk.
With beauty all around me, I walk.
It is finished in beauty. It is finished in
    beauty.
It is finished in beauty. It is finished in
    beauty.

The dance begins.

SINGERS

The corn comes up, the rain descends.
Vegetation comes.
The rain descends, the corn comes up.
The pollen comes.
Above it thunders,
His thoughts are directed to you,
Now to your house
Approaches for you.
He arrives for you.
He comes to the door,
He enters for you.
Behind the fireplace
He eats from his ceremonial dish.
"Your body is strong,
Your body is now holy," he says.

The dawn arrives and the singing ends with the Finishing Song.

SINGERS

From the pools in the green meadow
He takes up his sacrifice,
With that he now heals.
With that your kindred thank you now.

The basket is turned upright and the drumstick is taken outside by an assistant, who pulls it apart, sprinkling pollen on the shreds of yucca leaves from which is was made, repeating in a low voice the benediction.

ASSISTANT

Thus will it be beautiful.
Thus walk in beauty, my grandchild.

The patient, facing east, inhales the breath of the dawn.

RITES OF THE SPIRITUAL BODY

THE PATIENT OF the Navajo Night Chant is not the victim of physical disease as we understand it in the West, nor is the Indian term "medicine" related to pathology as Western physicians conceive of it. Indian medicine is spiritual and ceremonial. The concept of medicine does not stop with the idea of a drug that cures someone who is ill or a process that heals wounds. It also includes the complex idea of *orenda*, the force and the spirit of the tribe as a whole. The individual is one facet of this spirit. Illness is caused by the disharmony of the individual or of the entire tribe with nature. This concept is one of the primary bases of tribalism for Indians, providing a supernatural view of medicine, society, and the individual. This viewpoint is far more pantheistic and holistic than anything non-Indians usually associate with Indian magic or witchcraft, let alone concepts like the Great Spirit and the happy hunting ground. In a similar way, medicine bundles are not simply mysterious medical charms in the "little black bag" of the Indian holy man, whom whites usually envision as a witch doctor. Medicine bundles, which consist of an assortment of objects and herbs, are symbols of a religious concept. It is in them that *orenda* dwells, a holy of holies transcending European ideas of black magic and alchemy. Most Indians are astonished that their rites are regarded by many whites as black magic or sorcery—designations Indians would apply to the prayers of white people for disaster to strike their enemies.

Among the Inuit, Paiute, and Shoshone there is only one central focus in religion and medicine: the shaman. Other tribes have different religious ideas. The ceremonies of the Pueblo, for instance, range from the shamanistic treatment of a specific "patient" to communal ceremonies devoted to the welfare of the entire

Carved Ojibwa medicine box, or tabernacle, for preserving the sacred feathers used in the meetings of the Grand Medicine Society.

group. Indians normally have a holistic attitude toward disease—so that death among the old is generally accepted as the natural outcome of being animal. Death is also considered natural in early childhood—an infant dies because the soul (*orenda*) did not become firmly connected to the self. Although death is accepted and not the subject of great and abiding fear, this does not mean that Indians do not mourn the loss of their people. Death among the young and strong is mysterious. It is inexplicable and terrible. It is therefore the concern of holy men and women and the main focus of their arts. All tribes recognize five supernatural causes of disease and death—possession by an evil force, breach of a taboo, loss of harmony with nature, witchcraft, and the invasion of the body or spirit by something alien and hostile. Among the hunting tribes the shaman is essentially a voyager—someone who falls into a trance and travels to the spirit world, where he discovers the cause for illness and troubles. Among the Navajo a hand trembler is able to determine the cause of an ailment and recommend a ceremonial cure, which is then performed by a curer who is known as a chanter. The hand trembler's diagnostic abilities arise from the joining of his forces with the force of the Gila Monster, who causes his arm and hand to shake and to locate an illness, much as a divining rod is said to indicate the location of water.

☆   ☆   ☆

Some inkling of the awesomeness of *orenda* can be gleaned from encounters with the way in which Indians act out their worldview in ceremonies and dances. If you agree with those who believe that action came before cognition in human development, then you will recognize in bodily movement humanity's most fundamental and expressive act. Primal peoples tend to idealize action as a magical force. There is substantial physiological basis behind this viewpoint. We are born with organs of perception that provide us with our only means of experiencing the world. These organs include not only the senses of smell, sight, hearing, taste, and touch but also a sense of balance and of rotation, which the semicircular canals in the inner ear reveal to us. In addition we possess a kinesthetic sense, which operates through receptors in our muscle tissues and through our sensitivity to pressure and texture and which helps us realize when we are moving and on what kind of surface we are moving. From birth we are taught to recognize the ways in which the movements of our bodies work for us practically: swimming, driving, typing, writing, eating. But bodily movement has other functions—and primal people are as aware of them as they are of the purely practical ways in which motion serves us. Every emotional state expresses itself in movements that are not necessarily utilitarian. The relationship between feeling and movement affects everything from the expression in our

At Zia Pueblo a sick boy is treated by five shamans in a ceremonial chamber of the Giant Society. The men, seated behind a row of fetishes, holding plumes and straws in their left hand and rattles in the right, exorcise the disease with chants. The white line separating the boy from the others is made of cornmeal. An altar board leans against the left wall and near the ceiling there appears to be a crucifix. The Giant Society is one of four major medicine societies that work together for the well-being of the people, uniting their efforts in serious situations. Their power is not innate but was given to them by supernatural animals. It is in the fetishes that this power resides. (1888-1889)

eyes to the flow of adrenaline in our bloodstream. In its most fundamental form this spontaneous link between feeling and movement is called dance—a direct, nonverbal, unreasoned assertion of emotional states expressed in universal forms through pure physical assertion. Dance is an extremely powerful force in human experience.

Beyond the purely expressive powers of movement there is also its highly contagious nature. Yawning is the most obvious example of such contagiousness. So is the desire to stretch when we see someone else stretching. Because of the inherent contagion of motion, which makes the onlooker feel in his or her own body the exertions of others, the dancer is able to convey nonverbally the most intangible experiences. The body is capable of communicating in its own bodily manner. When one considers how powerfully movement influences us, it isn't difficult to understand why Indians regard an action as the embodiment of a mysterious force. They believe that dance can shape the circumstances of nature if it can focus its contagious power on animals and divinities. This premise is at the root of most ceremonial uses of dance.

The imitation of an animal (essentially in movements but also in costume) has a magical influence on the animal itself. This practice, which is called "homeopathic ritual," is the basis of most hunting and fertility rites. It probably resulted from a long history of less complex uses of bodily motion until it was determined that actions depicting the pursuit and slaying of an animal might assure success in the hunt. Indians generally think of animals as possessing superior powers to people, for Indians do not consider themselves the center of the universe or the special creatures intended to dominate the world.

✻ ✻ ✻

Since the Indian concept of life is based largely on movement rather than form, the transformation of one thing into another is not extraordinary. In many tribes it is believed that animals, and sometimes people, are capable of changing their outward forms quite easily. The world does not consist of inanimate materials and living things; *everything* is living and everything can therefore be of help or cause harm. That is the basis for the ceremonial relationship of human beings to nature. Indians have none of the cosmic egotism of Western civilization, which sees humanity as the crowning achievement of evolution. Nor do Indians possess the intolerance of nature that regards it essentially as a wilderness that requires the civilizing influence of humanity's superior mentality.

The people of North America do not think of their relationship to nature (and whatever power created it) as special, and therefore they do not believe themselves responsible to powers or divinities to make great sacrifices and payments for the favors bestowed upon them. The relationship between the Indians and the super-naturals has always been drastically different from what it is in most other cultures. Among Indians there is far more emphasis upon a friendly exchange than on the kind of supplication and humility that marks most religious rites. In general, offerings are made in the form of "gifts." They are tokens that recall the relationship of equals and of friends, one spirit and the other human. The use of smoke from the sacred pipe of the Plains tribes is important in the communication of powers. In the Southwest sacred beings and objects are "fed" with pollen or cornmeal.

Deer dancers, with their characteristic costume, black face paint, antlers, and sticks representing forelegs, are seen here with the Wild Turkey Woman and the buffalo dancers at San Ildefonso Pueblo, New Mexico. (1946)

Ceremonies involving animal dances are common.
This painting by George Catlin portrays the Bull Dance of
the Mandan Okipa Festival.

"Sometimes at night," Eddy Box (Red Ute) once whispered to me as we peered into the darkness of the medicine tepee where I had come to talk to him, "sometimes you can see them in there—like glowing lights, moving very rapidly. You can see them and you can hear them. And then it is time for the buffalo to come from the great distance. You can hear his hooves approaching until they are very loud. Very loud! And then he comes from up above, descending until his hooves are on the ground and you can see the steam of his ferocious breath and hear his heavy breathing. For he has come a long way from the other place."

Animals are considered to be as much involved with their own capture and death as are the weapons used against them. Animals form a loose supernatural society of their own. They have clans, and when they are away from human company they remove their fur skins and look very much like people. There is still among Indians an idea of animals that obliges a hunter to please an animal spirit in much the same manner that he might please himself. The hunters offer tokens and praise in order to gain the consent of the animals to kill one or two of their kind out of need for food. Among farmers and food gatherers there is a conviction that the earth is a spirit that controls plant life and the abundance of harvests and must therefore be treated ritualistically. The sea and its harvest are regarded in the same way by coastal peoples.

These animistic beliefs, this reverence for the spirits, the *orenda* within all things, and the need to propitiate these forces give rise to rituals, ceremonial dances, and the use of magic. The basis of Indian ceremony is the process of creating favorable relations with the spiritual forces of the earth, the sea, and the animal world. A striking feature of Indian culture is the pervasiveness of belief in these supernatural forces and in the physical world and the real body as the organs of spirituality.

The calumet, or sacred pipe, is first held stem to sky so that the One Above may be the first to smoke. Then the user, in this case an Oglala Sioux, sends puffs of smoke in the four directions. The buffalo skull is a sign of the necessary sacrifice of life and a token of the covenant between humanity and nature.

The Apache Mountain Spirit Dance

AMONG THE Apache the gan, or mountain spirits, are similar to the Navajo yei and the Hopi kachinas. The gan brought agriculture to the Apache. Once they lived with ordinary people, but as they wished to escape death they left and found a world of their own where life is eternal. Apache dancers impersonate the gan at numerous ceremonies. The most elaborate and important of these ceremonies is the Girls' Puberty Rite. The White-Painted Woman instructed the Apache in this ritual, and the young initiates identify with her during the annual summer ceremony that celebrates the girls' puberty. The Mountain Spirit Dance is performed during each night of the ceremony.

Because it is expensive, the ceremony is not now observed by all Apache families. A shaman must be hired to conduct the rites, as well as gan impersonators, who are central to the ceremony. In addition, large quantities of food must be provided for the vast group that assembles, since the ritual is also a major social event.

On the first day of the ceremony a ritual tepee composed of four spruce saplings is constructed. This skeletal tepee will house the young girl throughout the ceremony.

A buckskin is placed on the floor of the tepee and the shaman offers chants while two initiates perform a simple dance within the framework of the spruce poles. Because the initiate possesses special curative powers during this important period in her life, her services are often sought by the infirm, who urge her to touch or massage their limbs. During this dance the girl attends anyone who is ill and comes to her for comfort.

The initiate is dressed in ceremonial garments made of buckskin stained or painted a bright yellow, the color of sacred pollen. Nowadays the buckskin dress is often replaced by a contemporary yellow frock. Here the girl is attended by her sponsor, an older woman of the tribe who performs the role of god-mother and often contributes heavily to the funding of the event.

Meanwhile, the Apache holy men, who will serve as gan impersonators, prepare the wand that will be carried by the initiate.

The initiate presents herself to the tribal shaman during the Kneeling Ceremony. During the four days of ritual she must observe many taboos: she must not smile or laugh, for this causes premature wrinkling; she must maintain powerful thoughts about her future, for the ceremony is symbolic of the whole life journey the girl will take.

As the initiate looks on, pollen is blessed with the ritual wand, which is decorated with ribbons and feathers.

On each of the four nights, impersonators of the gan, or mountain spirits, bless the Apache encampment and drive away any evil that attempts to intrude upon the proceedings. First the shamans who will serve as gan dancers purify themselves in the sweat lodge.

After their purifying sweat bath the shamans then cleanse themselves in the river.

There are usually four gan dancers and one sacred clown, but the number may vary as high as sixteen, depending on the lavishness of the ceremony. At dusk they appear in traditional headdresses, garments, and body paint. They enter the dance ground, approach the central fire and the ceremonial tepee four times, and offer blessings to the initiate and to the tribe. A chorus and drummer accompany the dancers with songs handed down from generation to generation.

The initiate, accompanied by gan dancers and the tribal shaman, stands in the ceremonial tepee holding the ritual wand.

The songs determine which of the gan dances will be performed—the short freestyle or the high-stepping dance. The dance is composed of short, jagged, and angular movements, as well as posturing and gesturing with the painted swordlike wands made of yucca that the gan carry in each hand. Here the gan dancers bless the initiate.

Finally the wand is planted in the ground, thus symbolizing the initiate's passage from girlhood to womanhood. The tepee is ceremonially dismantled and the guests depart. The family remains alone at the camp until the ninth day, when the girl is purified by a bath in yucca suds. She is then a woman of her tribe, eligible for marriage. "The woman will walk happily upon the path of pollen."

THE COSMIC CONTRARY

CONTEMPORARY DANCES of American Indians are the most visible aspects of an enduring tradition. Of a more complex and less visible nature is the kachina world of the Southwest, a pantheon of more than two hundred and fifty spirits, best known to non-Indians in their individual iconographic form of kachina dolls, small painted and decorated figures carved from wood. Many of the kachinas represent the powers of entirely abstract ideas that are not easily conveyed to those not immediately involved in Pueblo culture. Others relate to the forces of plants, animals, birds, and beings from Pueblo history. The most organized kachina ritual is found among the Hopi and Zuni, but individual forms, also called kachinas, are the focus of the ceremonies of all the pueblos of New Mexico; for example, Ceremony of the Rain Powers of San Juan Pueblo.

Kachina dolls are presented to children by the kachina themselves. The dolls are learning tools to help the children identify the various divinities and are not sacred objects. But the members of tribal societies who impersonate the kachinas in ceremonial events are sacred. Once they don their costumes, paraphernalia, and masks, they become reflections of the powers of kachinas and may not be touched or involved in conversation or any other human exchange.

There are both male and female kachinas; however, the masked impersonators in ceremonies are always male, impersonating both male and female divinities. The sacredness of kachinas does not obstruct their potential for the grotesque, the outrageous, and the highly humorous. All such qualities are present in the great sacred dramas of Indians. The ceremonies are profoundly lucid in their seriousness and also in their ridiculousness—elements that rarely share the same values in other cultures as they do among Indians.

Representation is a complex relationship between reality and the symbols used to depict it. The *mili*, representing the breath-of-life given by Awonawilona, the supreme being of the Zuni, is envisioned as a perfect ear of corn, filled with seeds of sacred plants, wrapped in buckskin, set in a base of basketry, and covered with feathers from various birds. This *mili* is a fetish. It holds more significance than any of the physical objects that compose it. The fetish contains a living force which, if treated properly and with respect and if ceremonially fed, will give help to its owners. Such a fetish may be owned by an individual, a clan, a secret society, or by an entire tribe. The Corn Mother of the Hako Ceremony of the Pawnee is an example of a fetish that is owned by the tribe. The visionary images painted on a Blackfoot shield, however, are personal guardians. Because such fetishes are seen as living forces, they must be cared for and ceremonially fed, usually with cornmeal in the Southwest and with tobacco smoke on the Plains. When not in use, fetishes are kept in special containers and in special dwellings. They must be protected.

Such symbols and metaphoric images—which fill the silences between conventional meanings and supplement the overt significance that words can convey—are intriguing aspects of ceremony and are the core of Indian religious life. Nothing can

The Hopi eagle kachina is called Kwa Kachina or Kwahu, and the impersonators of this kachina sometimes appear at night ceremonies in March or during the Bean-Planting Festival. The carved wooden dolls are not sacred; they are created as a learning aid for Hopi children, who must memorize the characteristic features of many different kachinas. The dolls, like this modern example, are also created for the art market.

The Eagle Dance, performed in the spring, is the residue of a rite central to the ceremonial life of all the Pueblos. The Eagle Dance dramatizes the relationship between human beings and the sky powers (the sun) and is maintained by the eagle as a conveyor of human aspirations. The eagle down represents the breath-of-life and the plumage is used in Curing Rites. Two young men are costumed as eagles in the dance—one as a male eagle, the other as a female—and together they emulate flight. As in many of the animal dances, it is usual for the drummers and singers to dress in the traditional costume of the Plains Indians. The dance is open to the public and is a favorite among the Pueblos of the Rio Grande.

This magnificent buffalo hide war-medicine shield is one of the most important surviving Crow articles. It belonged to the great Chief Arapoosh at the time of the Lewis and Clark expedition. The design represents the Moon, which came to the owner in human form during a vision and gave him this shield. It was used as a talisman. When rolled along the ground, success was assured if it stopped face up, but if it fell face down, the project would be abandoned as foredoomed to failure.

adequately explain the meaning of a poetic metaphor. And nothing can make an "intelligible" experience out of an illogical but significant symbol, fetish, or ceremonial act. That is the reason for the inclusion in this book of actual ritual texts. They tell us nothing—but they suggest everything. Ignoring the world of objects that has been so excessively described to us in Western literature, the creative power of Indian rituals is their capacity to evoke, to produce images, to compound mystery with more mystery, and to illuminate the unknown without reducing it to the commonplace.

Among Indians there is a predominant quest for a personal vision which, once attained, becomes a vehicle and an embodiment of one's personal power. Indians are extremely observant, a result of childhood instruction among a people whose survival depended upon the most accurate and sensitive observations of nature and its subtle changes. But Indians also recognize the value of the night, when one must learn to see with more than the eyes.

Many white people deplore ambiguity and strive to clarify everything. Most Indians, however, strive for ambiguity in the form of metaphors and symbols. Indians thrive in the shadows. They can see the world out of the corner of their eye. There is so much in the world that slips past us when all we see is what is before us and is well defined. There are things that Indians learn not to look upon directly because they either disappear or change when seen squarely and clearly. It is usually deplorable in Western culture to concede that some things are unexplainable.

Though the sacred clowns and kachinas of the Southwest are not at once recognizable as universal figures in American Indian ceremonial life, they can be found in the rites of every tribe in various guises. Every initiated child of the Southwest villages knows that kachinas are men of the pueblo dressed in kilts, paints, feathers, and masks, but this does not detract from the fact that they nonetheless possess great and exceptional power. The credibility of kachinas is not based on the belief in their actual physical reality any more than the power of a painting requires

A women's dance, which the Navajos call Entah or Enemy Way, was once a purification rite for warriors. It is now performed for patients whose sickness is diagnosed as the result of contact with non-Indians. On the third and last day of the ceremony the black dancers (clowns of the rite) perform a Mud Dance during which the patient is dunked in a mud hole to loosen the grip of the evil causing his illness. After the patient has been treated the spectators of the event become fair game for the clowns, who catch them and dump them into the mud bath as well. (1925)

The sacred clowns. With hair tied in horns and decorated with cornhusk the koshare and kurena of the Rio Grande Pueblos possess the curiously meaningful bizarre appearance and perform the outrageous pranks of characters from a late Fellini film — the only form in Western culture which quite grasps the imposing otherness of the clowns and their profound impact upon our sensibilities.

us to believe that it is something other than paint and canvas. The men who impersonate kachinas are somewhat like art—merely the physical material in which something nonphysical is implemented. Kachinas are like figures in our dreams—illogical, unreal as far as waking reality is concerned, but absolutely convincing and curiously significant.

It is entirely appropriate in the scheme of Indian religious eloquence for a kachina to manifest itself in either the dignified gestures and sounds of Hastsheyalti (Talking Power) or the cavorting and ranting of a clown. Both divinities—serious and comic—are mythic powers having little relationship to commonplace reality, and both are magical in their impact and relationship to their initiates. There is paradox and duality in these irreconcilably opposite divinities only if one sees them as irreconcilable and opposite. Indians do not do so, and this aspect of their holistic attitude is both unique to them, as far as I can tell, and almost entirely beyond the comprehension of outsiders, including ethnologists who have spent several decades trying to resolve the rationale of the sacredness and the "obscenity" of the clowns that are central figures in many tribal ceremonies.

"You must learn to look at the world twice," Indian elders advise. "First you must bring your eyes together in front so you can see each droplet of rain on the grass, so you can see the smoke rising from an ant hill in the sunshine. *Nothing* should escape your notice. But you must learn to look again, with your eyes at the very edge of what is visible. Now you must see dimly if you wish to see things that are dim—visions, mist, and cloud people, animals which hurry past you in the dark. You must learn to look at the world twice if you wish to see all that there is to see."

The ability to envision a second world is a major source of an Indian knowledge so deeply felt, so primal, that it is neither word nor outcry, neither sign nor symbol but the ineffable *thing* itself, that which precedes speech and thought, that which is the raw experience itself without evaluation and moralities. It is the ineffable structured into an event—that which we call ritual. And what, after all, is this mysterious event that has eluded the Western world? It is an appearance—an apparition, if you like—that springs from what we do but not from what we are. It is something else. In watching a ritual, you do not see what is physically before you. What you see is an interaction of forces by which something else arises. Those who see only what is before them are blind. Ritual requires us to *really* see. What we are able to see if we use our eyes without censorship and prejudgments is a virtual image. It is real, for when we are confronted by it, it really does exist, but it is not actually there. The reflection in a mirror is such a virtual image; so is a rainbow. It seems to stand on earth or in the clouds, but it really "stands" nowhere. It is only visible, but it is not tangible. It is the unspeakable, the ineffable made visible, made audible, made experiential.

A fascination with the absurd is an important embodiment of paradox in both Native American and Asian philosophy. Cosmic contrariness is ritualized by a variety of sardonic figures in the Indian world. Besides the sacred clowns of the American Southwest, there are also numerous societies of "fools" among Plains, Northeastern, and Northwest Coastal tribes. Their costumes and dances are greatly varied, but their power as archetypal figures is universal.

"Many people who know about these things say that the clown is the most powerful," an Apache has commented when asked about the comic role of the sacred clown in ceremonies. "People think that the clown is just nothing, that he is just for fun. That is not so."

The clown exists in almost every Indian culture of North America. The Dakota clown is called a heyoka, a person who has been given the greatest possible vision, that of the Thunder Being. After this experience the Thunder Being "wears" the heyoka in a manner not unlike the way a holy man wears a sacred object around his neck. While worn by the Thunder Being, a new heyoka reverses his behavior, speaking contrarily, riding backwards on his horse, and doing everything in the opposite manner from his normal behavior. People look upon the heyoka with amusement and respect, for he represents a contradiction which Indians grasp as fundamental to life. The extraordinary is generally condemned and loathed by deeply traditional people, but Indians regard the extraordinary person as awesome. They accept perversity as a significant quality. Among whites the freak is a pitiful target of ridicule, since white culture disdains oddity and views all difference as peculiar and irrational. As Lame Deer perfectly expressed it, the Indian has a far more diversified metaphysical viewpoint: "Fooling around, a clown is really performing a spiritual ceremony." The clown's behavior is a visualization of his knowledge of *another reality*.

The clown is also found among the people of the North West Coast, who do not open their religious ceremonies until all the people, especially strangers, have laughed. The Arapaho Crazy Dancers evoke as much annoyance as they do humor, and so do the Cahuilla Funny Men of Southern California, and the members of the famous Iroquois False Faces. Clowns produce laughter and annoyance, but they also provoke fear; the Assiniboin clowns are avoided, and so are the Navajo clowns. "When they approach too closely," according to anthropologist Robert Lowie, "the smiles of the women and children quickly change to expressions of surprise, tempered with fear." Apache children are terrified by clowns, since they are known to carry bad children away in their baskets and eat them. The Fool Dancers of the Kwakiutl are said to have indulged in practical joking with such fury that they occasionally killed people.

The Fool Dance of the Assiniboin was a rare masked dance of the Plains tribes. Two Boys, the leader of the dancers, and one of his assistants pose for a photograph. Two Boys' costume and mask are made of canvas, and the dress is patterned after a woman's fringed garment. He carries a rattle-staff with dew claws of deer hanging from it and has a bone whistle in his mouth. (1906)

During the six-day Midwinter Ceremony of the Iroquois, False Faces visit each house in the community to extinguish the fire in each stove, stir the ashes, and blow them onto the inhabitants as a curative rite. Before a False Face troupe enters a house, one of them opens the door, rubs his turtle-shell rattle against the wooden doorjambs, makes the characteristic inhuman False Face cries, and then closes the door. Only at this point can the group enter, crawling toward the stove. A member of the household begins to beat a stick on a bench and sing, and the False Face Dance is performed. The False Faces rub their hands in the ashes and hot coals in the stove but do not suffer burns. They make use of every opportunity to play pranks. Then they run off.

Kwakiutl are said to have indulged in practical joking with such fury that they occasionally killed people.

All clowns possess complete liberty, from the contraries of the Cheyenne to the neweekwe clowns of the Zuni. Their targets of ridicule are themselves as well as others. But they also turn their comedy upon shamans and other high religious authorities. The Navajo clown participates in the Mountain Chant by burlesquing the sacred sleight-of-hand tricks of the ceremony, revealing their secrets and disrupting the ritual with laughter and ridicule. There is little in Western culture that provides a parallel to such antics, unless we look at the theatre of the absurd, where we discover in the characters of Samuel Beckett and Eugene Ionesco people for whom the bizarre, the irrational, the comic, and the tragic are utterly compatible.

Members of the Zuni neweekwe, or Galaxy Fraternity, are shamans who care for the sick with the use of magic and invocation. Initiates into the secret society were required to undergo experiences such as eating human excrement. (1909)

The plays of the absurd dramatize the horror of metaphysical irrationality in grotesque dialogue and actions—a rather apt description of at least some aspects of the performance of the sacred clown. The contemporary cinema also offers appropriate parallels to the mockery of the clowns. A filmmaker like Ingmar Bergman reminds people that his cinematic tricks are not in themselves the power that produces film art but are instead a symbolic demonstration of aesthetic power, which of itself is ineffable. This is very much like the technique of the Navajo clown who clumsily reveals the secrets of the sacred sleight-of-hand tricks. He forces people to look at everything twice—first, seeing the apparent acts and implements of religious life and, then, *seeing* the invisible power behind the sleight-of-hand tricks, which is the basis of all ceremonial life and of all "realities."

The shock techniques of dadaism and the late films of Federico Fellini have a great deal in common with the contrariness of sacred clowns, especially those of the Southwest. In the 1880s Adolph Bandelier visited Cochiti Pueblo and made notes that resemble the outraged journalism of conservative film critics of Fellini's cinema: "The whole is a filthy, obscene affair. They were drinking urine out of bowls and jars used as privies on the house tops, eating excrements and dirt."

Clowns are poor—or at least that is their disguise. Everywhere in North America the costume of the clowns is rags. They frequently beg for food or, if necessary, steal it, though no one ever stops them from taking whatever they want. "They are very dangerous, and whoever refuses them food will be injured." This same aggression also applies to their attitude toward sex. They talk, sing, and joke about it constantly. They enact sexual displays that might be shocking in other societies and that would be equally unusual among the normally modest Indian tribes were it not for the special liberty granted clowns. Before the missionaries the Pueblo clowns wore enormous dildos and often exhibited themselves. Bandelier's diary expresses his shock when witnessing a Cochiti ceremony: "They chased after her, carried her back and threw her down in the center of the plaza, then while one was performing the coitus from behind, another was doing it against her head. Of course, all was simulated, and not the real act, as the woman was dressed. The naked fellow performed masturbation in the center of the plaza or very near it, alternately with a black rug and his hand. Everybody laughed."

The report of Bandelier expressed shock and dismay, a response of many ethnologists who fortunately put aside their repulsion and recorded these clown rites in the era prior to their repression (c. 1920) by the Bureau of Indian Affairs and Protestant missionaries. There was a period when art critics were equally perplexed by the sexuality of novels and films of their own societies; in fact, a preoccupation with criticism of obscenity has been so distracting that most critics missed the philosophical and artistic achievements of writers like James Joyce and D. H. Lawrence. Today, however, the concept of sexuality as a vital, expressive vehicle for nonsexual ideas is no longer peculiar or strange to Christians and Jews. Post-Freudian ideas about sex have extended into politics and metaphysics, assuming a metaphoric vitality that makes possible the expression of ideas and values previously inaccessible to Western culture. Whites finally recognized that there is expressiveness in sexual imagery which goes beyond the notion of sex as an obscene joke, or a fertility symbol, or antisocial behavior. The American Indian's sacred clown has for centuries epitomized the vitality of perversity, humor, sexuality, aggressiveness, and absurdity—an act possible only for those beyond duality and dichotomies of flesh and spirit, sacred and profane, individual and tribal.

The role of the individual in the society of the dominant white culture is so much taken for granted that it is extremely difficult to realize how differently Indians see themselves in relation to the tribal group. In a very important way the clown represents the birth of the idiosyncratic—or, as white people would probably see it, the birth of the *individual*. Normally *orenda*—the tribal power—is essentially a group soul, which is manifested in each baby as it is born into the tribe and which is carried through life and death, when it passes back to the tribe. It is a concept

Zuni sacred clowns—mudheads—laze in the late afternoon sun at the conclusion of the Rain Dance. Their bodies are painted with red clay, and except for the black woolen scarf worn around their necks, they are nude. The modesty of the clowns facing the camera, but not those in view of the Pueblo people, is clearly at the suggestion of the photographer. (1899)

entirely remote from the individualized soul imagined by Christians and other sects. The sacred clown, however, appears to alter this unity of the tribe relationship to the communal and nonindividual power of *orenda*. Usually the members of the tribe are not special, their power is not essentially individual, nor does it possess any individuating characteristics. Their "souls" are community property, especially among the tribes of the Southwest, which are very conservative and extremely conformist— the individual (at least as the whites understand the word) has little value to Southwest Indian society. The Plains tribes, on the other hand, are involved in vision quests that are quite individualized, resulting in visions that are personally owned and can even be sold to others who do not attain vision.

But there is really nothing in Indian tribal life that begins to approximate the Western concept of individuality and free will. It follows that Indian societies do not provide a place for individuals and therefore do not provide the regulations that govern the limits of individuality. Whites are devoted to limiting the rights of individuals and preventing anarchy, which is greatly feared by individualized cultures. By contrast the Indian, generally speaking, does not recognize the individual and therefore has not formulated strict regulations for his or her control. The thrust of the ego in the individual is so slight a threat to Indian tribes that common gossip and ceremonialized ridicule is generally sufficient to keep people living together harmoniously. Because individualism was viewed from an entirely different standpoint by Indians than it was by whites, idiosyncratic behavior, perversity, and actions that were highly deviant and nonconformist were not looked upon as a demonstration of madness or as the threat of anarchy or the expression of heresy. Such peculiar behavior was often seen by Indians as a manifestation of spirituality. The clowns were permitted to be exceptional. Anyone in the tribe who was perverse was automatically provided with a significant rather than a degrading role in the society.

As a group the clowns represent the rise of a unique sort of individuality in Indian tribes, possessing the extraordinary power, the privilege, the license, and the expressive freedom denied everyone else. As we witness the role assigned to clowns in ceremonies and in tribal life, we see clearly the ways in which they assume a function for Indians similar to the saints, the prophets and, especially, the artists of the white world; they are those whose specialness provides a human connection between the accessible and the inaccessible. Ultimately these outsiders, these clowns and contraries, symbolize the act of initiation which raises people from the commonplace and gives them access to the extraordinary. As the people of Acoma Pueblo say of their first clown: "He knew something about himself."

The Cherokee Booger Dance

THE BIG COVE BAND of the Eastern Cherokee lives in a land of frozen mountain slopes, deep ravines, and chilling torrents, where severe and long winters curtail the growing season and isolate these tenacious Southeastern Indians. Such difficult conditions and the fact that the Eastern Cherokee hid out and resisted the Removal of 1835 (which relocated the Five Civilized Tribes in the Indian territory now called Oklahoma) has made them a sturdy reservoir of old-time life-styles. But isolation and tenacity may not entirely account for the Cherokee cultural persistence. In the famous Booger Dance-Drama at Big Cove there is perhaps more to be found than a persistent ceremonial antique that has survived in an isolated geographical pocket of the Great Smoky Mountains.[2]

In this ritual, which is not quite the same as any other Cherokee ceremony, we discover a dramatic record of the anxiety of the tribe, a strong reaction against the symbol of the invaders, and an expression of insecurity and fear in dealing with the white world that surrounds the Big Cove settlement. It has been suggested that the Booger Dance fuses the invasion of the white people to the spiritual forces of nature with which the Cherokee learned to cope and therefore makes the existence of whites somehow less threatening and alien to tribal experience. The Cherokee believe that they cannot deal with the white invaders as a majority with political power, but when the same white people are transformed into mythical animals and grotesquely obscene creatures the Indians feel competent to cope with them in terms of ceremony—the means by which, at a much earlier time, they transmuted their harsh geographical environment into a familiar ritual context

through which they could assert influence and ultimately achieve harmony.

The Booger Dance-Drama perfectly ritualizes an extremely ugly and difficult experience of the Cherokee of Big Cove. It describes the coming of outsiders intruding into the midst of tribal life uninvited, seeking something to exploit. In the drama these mountain people tolerate the invaders until, the exploits gratified, the whites leave. Thus the white people's existence, their unmannerly insistences and intrusion into the Cherokee home circles at the height of social festivities, become marvelously grotesque aspects of a ritual experience called the Booger Dance.

The term "booger"—equivalent of "bogey"—is used by English-speaking Cherokee and their white neighbors for any ghost or frightful animal. The participants or boogers of the ceremony are a company of four to ten masked men representing "people from far away or across the water." Each masked dancer has a personal name, usually "obscene" by white standards and intended as ridicule. This name is given upon request to the host of a house party into which the masked dancers come noisily and uninvited. The boogers represent various European people. They pretend to speak languages other than Cherokee, and then only in whispers exclusively to the host of the ritual party. They cough, clear their throats, growl, and move with great awkwardness. Their masks represent Europeans with exaggerated features: bushy eyebrows, mustaches, whiskers, big noses, ghastly white pallor, and bald heads—distinguishing characteristics not often found among Indians. Boogers sometimes transform their bodies by stuffing their abdomen, buttocks, and shins. Some carry an imitation phallus made of a gourd neck concealed beneath a quilt or sheet that is worn as a costume. They perform diabolical grossness in their imitation of sex-seeking whites, exposing the gourds when dashing toward women and girls. Often the gourd-phallus contains water, which is sprayed everywhere with the exaggerated antics of a burlesque clown.

[2]Major source: Frank G. Speck and Leonard Broom, *Cherokee Dance and Drama*, 1951.

The names of the boogers lend a dramatic impact to their individual antics. These names, usually translated euphemistically by ethnologists, are intended to be brazen, insulting, and grotesquely humorous: Black Ass, Big Balls, Sooty Ass-Hole, Rusty Ass-Hole, Prick, Long Dong, Sweet Meat, Big Rectum, Her Cunt Has Long Hairs. There is a category of conventional "obscene" names for boogers, although original appellations, when appropriate to the ribald spirit of the ritual, are much applauded. The one or two women masked as females who occasionally form part of the booger gang are not called upon to give a solo clown dance as are the men whether masked as men or women. The women sit on a bench until the final dance movement of the ceremony, and afterward they join all the other masked dancers who take part.

There seems to be no religious symbolism in the function of the Booger Dance-Drama among the Eastern Cherokee, whatever its origins or original intentions (which some ethnologists see as a winter rite to frighten away ghosts and evil spirits). Unlike the Iroquoian false faces the boogers' masks are not initially carved from a living tree to imbue them with life, nor are they ceremonially fed or referred to as "grandfathers," or offered tobacco, rubbed with grease, kept face upward, or protected from ridicule. However, the masks are taboo to pregnant women, which suggests that the Eastern Cherokee regard them as powerful.

PRELUDE

THE GUESTS of a Cherokee house party perform social dances or one of the usual night series of animal dances of the tribe. The people pretend they know nothing of what will follow, but an atmosphere of excitement and expectation builds for an hour or more.

First Action

SUDDENLY the booger gang, led by a spokesman, boisterously barges into the house. The maskers are systematically malignant. On entering, one of them immediately breaks wind noisily, and the guests respond with great applause and laughter. Another booger falls to the floor and then leaps madly to his feet, hitting the spectators and pushing people around while in pursuit of fleeing girls. After a good deal of rowdy behavior, farting, noisemaking, and sexual mime, the boogers are seated on a bench along the wall.

Second Action

THE HOST of the house party invites everyone to be seated and to be quiet. Then he asks who is the leader of the maskers. The spokesman is noisily pointed out by the gang of boogers. Now the host talks in whispers with the leader, asking him who the visitors are, where they have come from, and where they are going. The host pretends to interpret the answers to his question for the house-party guests, who act as if they were surprised that the maskers are from distant lands and are going to more distant places. Next the host asks the boogers what they want. The response is always decisive and candid: "Girls!" And the host explains, "They want girls. Oh! They are really after them! Chase them around!" To all of this the party guests act surprised and unhappy.

Besides wanting girls, the boogers usually also indicate to the host that they want "to fight." But the house-party host insists that Indians are very peaceable people and do not want to fight. Failing an agreement to fight or get girls, the booger leader indicates that his gang would like to dance. To this the Cherokee host emphatically agrees and the guests applaud. Before the dances begin, however, the host tells the boogers that the house guests would like to know who these strangers are by name. This leads to the following Rabelaisian game.

Third Action

THE LEADER of the boogers whispers his mask-name to the host, and the host announces the name aloud, to the delight of the guests. No one is ever quite certain what imaginative new name may be given for one of the several traditional masks worn by the boogers. The more obscene the name the greater the laughter.

Then the singers of the house party, four to ten in number, the head singer with a drum, begin the Booger Dance song. The song is repeated four times while each booger performs a solo dance, stamping emphatically with both feet, bending forward, hopping alternately on the right and the left foot. The dance is theatrically grotesque and awkward, like a clumsy white man trying drunkenly to imitate an Indian dance step. The first line of the song uses

Cherokee booger masks occur in a variety of sizes and shapes. Depicted here is a mask of an Indian woman (ca. 1920-1930)

the name of each booger who dances, and each time the name is sung the guests shout and applaud.

One by one the boogers perform their solo dances, until all have competed in drawing applause and laughter with their outrageous names and antics. This clowning is pantomimic rather than vocal. The boogers constantly dash headlong into the corner where the women and children are seated, pulling up their sheets and thrusting their buttocks out and exhibiting their concealed gourd-phalli. After these frantic exhibitions the host of the party asks in a whisper if the maskers would like to join the party in a dance. The boogers' leader replies that they would like to dance a Bear Dance or Eagle Dance or Pigeon Dance, also permissible in this interlude).

INTERLUDE

THE SINGERS of the house party sing a song in which the word *ats-legi-ss-ki*, "smokes," dominates. The host fills and lights a pipe—tradition calls for a pipe of stone made in native style by the Cherokee. He takes one puff himself, facing the fire and with his back to the boogers. Then he holds the pipe to the mouth of the drummer and each of the singers, giving each a puff—the smoke that rises from their nostrils signifying the breath-of-life. Now the host puts the pipe aside.

Fourth Action

THE BEAR DANCE begins. The dancers circle counterclockwise. A number of women dancers, equal to the number of boogers, join the dance line during the second song of the dance. One woman wears turtle-leg rattles and partners the booger leader. The entry of these nicely dressed women symbolizes the submission of the Indian to the will of the invaders. Erotic display is rather overt in the Bear Dance. As soon as the women enter the dance the boogers begin exhibiting themselves sexually. They close upon the women from behind and perform movements simulating intercourse. They uncover large gourd-phalli and thrust them at their partners. The women ignore them and dance serenely. The boogers shuffle and sway, emulating the actions of a bear.

When the dance is over, the boogers exit noisily to continue on their mysterious journey. While they exit, some boogers race clumsily among the women and try to drag off a struggling victim. The women laugh and the girls scream. The boogers finally give up and dash off into the night.

With the disappearance of the maskers, the Booger Dance-Drama ends. The house party now continues happily with performances of traditional dances without any further interruption by the boogers or any other brutish ghosts of the invaders.

The Hopi Holy Cycle

THE COURSE of Hopi cosmology—the Road of Life—unfolds each year in a cycle of nine great religious ceremonies that dramatize the Pueblo laws of life. As Frank Waters has suggested, no other folk art in North America compares with the poetry and complexity of these profound mystery plays. "They wheel slowly and majestically through the seasonal cycles, like the constellations which time their courses and imbue their patterns with meaning.... Even their names seem derived from an ancient and cryptic mythology known only to the mirroring stars above: Wuwuchim, Soyal, Powamu, Lakon, Owaqlt—words unknown to us, perhaps, but great names of great things, old names, as old as the shape of America itself."[3]

In the Hopi ceremonial cycle the earth, the people and the sky are intricately blended into a consciousness that precedes and predates theology, astronomy, and geography. The Hopi people say of the twin peaks called San Francisco that they are "our mother; we nurse from these peaks for religious survival." This is but one example of the way that the land, the human psyche, and the cosmic seasons operate in perfect balance for the Hopi mind. All things are connected to the center.

Barton Wright has observed that "the rich tapestry of Hopi ceremonial life is interwoven by the belief that nature and God are one and that the universe is totally reliable if properly approached."[4] In that cosmos, every force and every object possesses a spirit which can be induced to mediate the various powers of the Hopi world—a world in which the natural and supernatural are unified into a balanced cosmos.

Many elements of the Hopi world are insubstantial, "substanceless shapes of [evanescent] mist, the physical world's mirror images."[5] Many other elements of life are concretized in the quasi-human form of the kachinas. These kachinas are power figures associated with the bringing of rain—an urgent concern of dry-farmers, an agricultural tradition that depends upon rainfall for the fertility of the fields. As we have already noted, kachinas are represented both in doll-like forms and by impersonators—Hopi men who believe that when they don the costumes and masks of the kachinas they are transformed by their ineffable power and, with appropriate songs and dances, are able to bring benefits to the tribe.

Throughout the year, a cycle of ceremonies is performed in honor of the major forces associated with central elements in the tribe's practical and spiritual life. Rites lasting nine to sixteen days honor the most powerful spirits, while a variety of other dances accompany the appearance of the kachinas. "These rituals are performed for many purposes—to insure that sufficient Hopi men are indoctrinated in their religious duties to carry out the necessary functions; to turn the sun back toward the Hopi country from its annual migration southward; to purify the villages or renew the world; and to ready the fields and children for fertility, growth, and fruition."[6]

For six months of the annual ceremonial cycle, the relatively brief kachina dances are interlaced with other, more important rites. The kachinas appear in the Hopi villages at the winter solstice, a few at a time. Their numbers and variety gradually increase until the summer solstice in mid-July when they "go home" to the Hopi otherworld.

Most of the rites and some of the kachina dances take place in the seclusion of the underground ceremonial chambers, or kivas, while most of the kachina dances are held in the plazas of the Hopi villages.

---

[3] Frank Waters, *The Book of the Hopi*, 1963.

[4] Barton Wright in *J. Mora, The Year of the Hopi*, Smithsonian Institution, Washington, D.C., 1979, p. 17.

[5] Ibid.

[6] Ibid., p. 18.

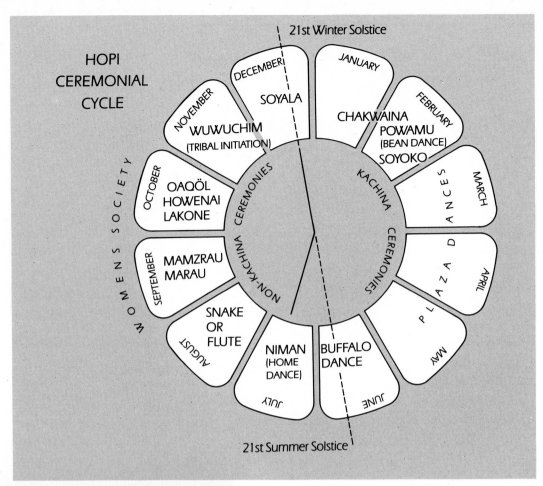

HOPI CEREMONIAL CYCLE

21st Winter Solstice

DECEMBER — SOYALA
NOVEMBER — WUWUCHIM (TRIBAL INITIATION)
OCTOBER — OAQÖL HOWENAI LAKONE
SEPTEMBER — MAMZRAU MARAU
AUGUST — SNAKE OR FLUTE
JULY — NIMAN (HOME DANCE)
JUNE — BUFFALO DANCE
MAY
APRIL
MARCH
FEBRUARY — CHAKWAINA POWAMU (BEAN DANCE) SOYOKO
JANUARY

WOMENS SOCIETY

NON-KACHINA CEREMONIES

KACHINA CEREMONIES

PLAZA DANCES

21st Summer Solstice

Inside the kiva of the One-Horned Priests, who guard the underworld from which the Hopi people originally emerged. Displayed are four baskets (plaques) filled with cornmeal and in which pahos (prayer sticks with feathers) are placed. The cornmeal is used to make a path for the guidance of humanity.

The Hopi ceremony cycle both begins and ends with the Wuwuchim, during which all Hopi men are initiated into one of the four sacred societies of the tribe. The Two-Horned Priests, seen here in their kiva, are members of one of these four societies, which are central to the activities of the ceremonial life of the Hopi.

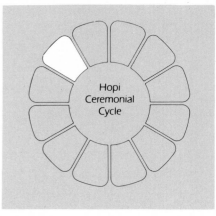

SOYALA

The Kachina Ma'na carries a ceremonial basket of
corn ears bound in a circle and resting on a bed of
spruce bows. The Hopi maiden on the left has a
squashblossom hairdo, showing that she has reached
the age of puberty.

Shortly after the Wuwuchim ceremony comes the Soyal, the celebration of the Hopi New Year, performed during the winter solstice. The ceremony marks the reappearance of the kachinas in the person of Ahulani, in the center, with his two sisters: Yellow Corn Girl and Blue Corn Girl. Their return heralds the return of the sun from its southward winter migration. During Soyal the village is ritually cleansed of its misfortunes and ills. Soyal celebrates the renewal of the world.

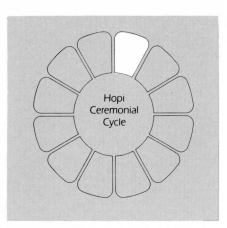

BUFFALO
DANCE

Following the Soyal there is a phase called Pamurti, a period of quiet during January and early February when quasi-social animal dances with a residue of ritualistic meaning, such as the Buffalo Dance, are performed in the plazas. Both men and women participate. The leader is usually dressed as a hunter, and there can be several different animals represented. These animals usually dance in two lines, with a woman between them. The woman wears a sun symbol bustle and she is called Buffalo Mother or Buffalo Woman and represents the mother of all animals. When she wears a simple feathered headdress she is called Wild Turkey Woman. This female dancer departs from the village at dawn and ritually leads the animal dancers into the plaza. These dances (usually eight cycles are performed before and after noon) are accompanied by drummers and a male chorus in Plains Indian costume, which had led to the assumption that the dance probably came from the northern Plains tribes. The ceremony ends with a symbolic "kill" and the limp bodies of the animal dancers are carried from the plaza. (1921)

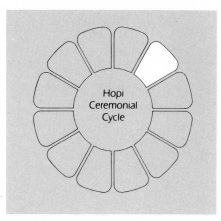

POWAMU
(BEAN DANCE)

The Powamu, or Bean-Planting Ceremony, is the first major event of the kachina ceremonial season. It is both a fertility rite and an initiation rite. In the fire-heated kivas beans are sprouted in boxes. The Powamu kachinas bless the sprouts, which are then passed out among the people. On the sixteenth day of Powamu young children are ritually whipped as part of their initiation rite. Then the kachinas remove their masks, revealing to the initiates that the kachinas are really human beings.

The fearsome Sokoyo rites take place during Powamu. The children of the village are terrorized by Ogre Woman and her hideous companions, who threaten to devour them until their families "buy" them back with food and promises of good behavior. Some of the Sokoyo kachinas are shown here (from left to right): Hahiwuqti, Watacka Naamu, Natacka Mana, Natackawuqti, Kutca Natacka, Mumbi Natacka, Kumbi Natacka, and three Heheas. (1893)

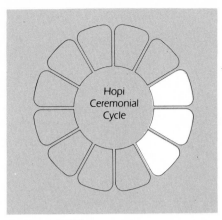

PLAZA DANCES

In late spring and early summer the famous Plaza Dances are held, during which the long lines of kachinas perform in the open plazas. Devoted to the power of the kachinas to bring rain, the Plaza Dances are of two types: Line Dances, in which the kachinas all wear the same mask and costume, and Mixed Dances, in which a variety of kachinas in various masks and costumes are represented.

Here the Ota line dancers are accompanied by Alo Mana, the White-Faced Kachina Girl, and a side dancer.

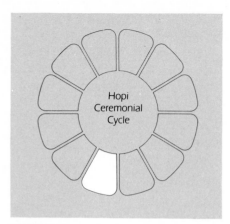

NIMAN
(HOME DANCE)

The Niman, or Home Dance, is a sixteen-day Hopi ceremony beginning just before the summer solstice. The final dance marks the best kachina rite of the season and the return of the kachinas to their homes. The Hemis kachinas, with elaborate, high tablitas, are usually favored for the Niman. Here we see the Hemis kachinas at the Hopi village of Shungopovi. (1901)

A major aspect of the Niman is the capture of eagles. They are tied to the rooftops and honored with gifts of tiny bows and arrows and flat kachina dolls.

The day after Niman is over, the kivas are ritually closed, and the eagles that have been captured and cared for are smothered.

The feathers of the eagle are plucked and used to construct pahos, plumed prayer sticks, that will be used in future ceremonies.

The bodies of the eagles are then buried with great respect and care. A miniature bow and arrow are placed on top of the grave.

There are ritual events after the departure of the kachinas and the closing of the kivas. Two such events are the Flute Dance and the famous Snake Dance, which alternate annually.

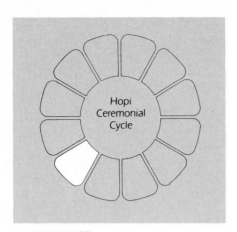

FLUTE DANCE

The Hopi Flute Ceremony is performed by the priests of the Blue and the Gray Flute Societies in August. The priest at the left is carrying a basket of sacred cornmeal. During the secret days of the ceremony the sand altar is made and at night songs are performed within the kivas. The public rites of the ceremony begin at the sacred spring where several men sit on the bank while a priest searches the water for three pottery jars containing fetishes. The two maidens at the far right and the boy, far left, represent ancestral heroes and their dress and facial makeup are traditional. On the ground, are the costumes and the sun shields used in this ceremony. (1902)

The Hopi then ascend to terraces and don their costumes. The men of Oraibi wear decorated kilts with a fox skin suspended at the back. The sun shield, made of buckskin that is stretched over a hoop and surrounded by eagle feathers and horsehair, is worn as a bustle. As the procession winds its way to the mesa top where the village is located, the group stops three times and cloud symbols are made with cornmeal on the ground just in front of the two maidens and the boy. Singing and the music of flutes accompanies the rites. The final rite of the Flute Ceremony is the gathering of men of the Gray Flute and Blue Flute Societies around a kisi, or shade house, of green branches. The leader and the boy carrying a water jar enter, and while the man prays the boy empties the water into the sipapuni (a small hole representing the place from which the people emerged from the underworlds). The music then ends and the ceremony is over. (1902)

The Snake Dance, like the Flute Ceremony, is a sixteen-day rite believed to have once been performed among all the Rio Grande Pueblos, though it survives today only among the Hopi. The ceremony ritualizes the journey of a Hopi youth who followed the upward course of the river now called the Colorado to find its source. With the aid of Spider Woman he eventually encountered the Great Snake, who rules all the waters of the world from his kiva. The youth was adopted by the Snake People and married a young girl who had been transformed into a snake. As a result of this alliance with the Snake People, the youth was given power by Spider Woman and designated Antelope Chief, instructor of his own people in the wisdom and ceremonies of the Snake People. The gathering of the snakes commences eight days before the public rites. Four days are spent hunting—one day in each of the cardinal directions. All snakes, poisonous and otherwise, are blessed and gathered. Altars and sand paintings are made in the kivas of the Snake and Antelope societies where secret rites are conducted. Each day the snakes are carried to the Snake kiva, where they are washed and purified. At sunrise on the eighth day the Antelope Race is held. Participants run to the village on top of the mesa. A cottonwood kisi is built in the plaza. A sipapuni is made in front of the kisi. Toward evening the Antelope men with gray body paint and the snake dan-

cers with reddish paint appear in the plaza and form two lines facing each other near the kisi. The Antelope men sing while the Snake men dance. The kisi is circled four times by the Antelope and Snake men, who are paired off. Each Antelope man reaches into the kisi and brings out a cornstalk, which he carries in his mouth while moving around the plaza. The cornstalk is handled as if it were a reptile. This same procedure is followed the next day, except the Snake men pair off and when one of them reaches into the kisi he brings out a snake. His partner, or "hugger," dances close by, distracting the reptile with his eagle-feather snake whip. One circuit is made with the snake in the dancer's mouth while the hugger strokes it with his snake whip. When each snake has been handled and danced around the plaza, the Snake and Antelope men gather the reptiles and form a circle. A ring of sacred cornmeal is made on the ground and all the snakes are thrown into it. Cornmeal is then sprinkled on the snakes and before they can escape they are grabbed by men, who race down the mesa to return the animals to their homes where they may act as messengers of the Hopi's prayers. After the snakes have been returned to the desert floor below the mesa, the performers of the ceremony drink an emetic made of herbs and beetle juice. The vomiting that follows consumption is part of the purification rite. The performers also bathe their bodies with the emetic.

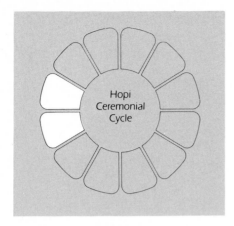

Hopi
Ceremonial
Cycle

WOMEN'S SOCIETY DANCES

Another cycle of events which take place after the departure of the kachinas are the ceremonies of the women's societies, such as the Oaqöle, Lakone, and Mamzrau, accompanied by dances, races, and gift giving. These ceremonies, which are held in September and October, emphasize both the harvest and certain herbal curative practices that are associated with women. Here the women of the Mamzrau perform a circle dance, stepping slowly to their right as they move prayer boards up and down.

Palhik Mana is the first to appear in the Mamzrau ceremonies. She is not a kachina for she is female and therefore may not impersonate a kachina in Hopi society. Palhik Mana appears as a group of four identically costumed figures, wearing one of the most elaborate coronets of the Indian Southwest. Her dances are among the most beautiful for their costume, high tablita, and movement.

The Lakone Ceremony, or Basket Dance as it is popularly known, is one of the most attractive of the women's society ceremonies. Its name is taken from the use of handsomely woven food baskets, which represent thanksgiving for the harvest of the earth. The dance is an epic of the Indian woman's life and glorifies her as the life-sustaining principle of the Pueblo.

In the afternoon the priestesses, each carrying a basket while chanting, form a circle in the plaza. The baskets, held in both hands, are slowly raised—first to one breast and then to the other—and then lowered to the groin. At the climax of the dance the young girls throw their baskets high in the air and the young men struggle for the prizes.

The Howenai, a scalp dance (victory dance) borrowed from the Pueblo peoples of the Rio Grande, has been transformed by the Hopi women's Mamzrau society into a Harvest Dance. The Howenai is one of several ceremonies the Mamzrau present every four years during their initiation rites.

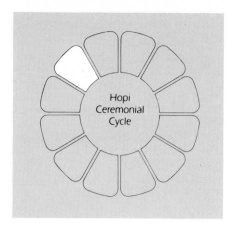

WUWUCHIM
(TRIBAL INITIATION)

The Hopi ceremonial year draws to a close with the Wuwuchim, during which young men are initiated into the sacred societies. Within sixteen days of the completion of the Wuwuchim, the Hopi prepare themselves for the New Year and a new season. Thus the Wuwuchim both closes and reopens the ceremonial cycle of the Hopi, And the ancient cycle of the holy days begins again.

The Tewa Rain-Power Ceremony

THE TEWA PUEBLOS are divided into moieties called Summer People and Winter People (or Pumpkin People and Turquoise People). Each moiety takes charge of the pueblo ceremonial life for its appropriate half of the year. Ritual surrounds the importance to these desert people of the cycle of vegetation and the activities of natural forces connected with dry agriculture (practiced without irrigation). The rain powers are therefore special spirits of immense importance. They are called the Great Ones and the Great Parents of all the people. The ritualistic contact between parents and children, rain powers and the people of the pueblos, is an essential aspect of the Tewa mentality and worldview.[7]

The ritual drama of the rain powers is acted out in the kiva, which is the ceremonial chamber of the Pueblo Indians, preserved for secret rites and restricted, at least in this century, to tribal members. Many Pueblo kivas are partially underground and round in construction, entered through an opening in the roof with the use of a ladder. In San Juan Pueblo, however, the kivas are rectangular in shape and adjacent to structures that are private homes. There is a nonceremonial kiva in San Juan that is used for public dances, and it is to this kiva only that non-Indians may be admitted.

The term "rain power" derives from the Hopi word *k'a-ci'nna*, or kachina, a term used to depict "those from over the horizon" among all the Pueblo peoples. Winter and Summer people have a different set of rain powers, each with its own name, wearing its own particular mask, and making individual sounds and gestures. Most of the rain powers carry yucca whips

or other sacred paraphernalia used in the ceremonies. Though the masks of the kachinas are individual, their dress is essentially the same. The masks are repainted for each ceremony, decorated with earrings of turquoise or mica slate and, where appropriate to the kachina, with elaborate feathers. The dancers are dressed in white shirts and white embroidered dance kilts that reach the knees. Long fringes hang down the back of the body from the handwoven sashes. White painted moccasins are worn along with white crocheted cotton leggings. Traditionally, garlands of spruce are placed around the waist and neck to conceal the lower rim of masks; spruce is also worn in bands around the arms. Under these costumes and masks the dancers' bodies are ceremonially painted.

The transformation of the dancer into the kachina is instantaneous and represents a unique and complex aspect of the Indian view of the impermanence of the apparent forms of things. As soon as the mask has been placed on a dancer, he immediately *becomes* a rain power. He cannot walk or talk like a human being any longer. He must not be touched by anyone. His movements become peculiar and highly expressive, though only the clowns and the caciques understand them and must, therefore, interpret the kachinas' movements for the assembled people.

The term "cacique" is taken from the Arawak term *kassequa*, meaning the religious leader of a moiety. During the ceremony the Winter and Summer caciques sit together in the kiva in the place of honor, directly in front of the people, who normally sit on the floor.

The clowns represent emotional and moral values totally removed from the ideas of Western civilization. They have bare chests, and their bodies are painted with black-and-white horizontal stripes. Instead of wearing masks, the clowns paint circles around their eyes and mouths and wear headdresses of skin and cornhusks. A small length of cotton fabric is tied around their hips and legs, covering only their groins. Attached to their moccasins are large rattles of turtle shell, which jingle when they move.

[7]Major source: Vera Laski, *Seeking Life*, 1958.

The ceremony also includes priestesses, who are elder members of the women's society. Other participants are virgin girls respected for their purity who may serve in the ceremony only once. The people (Children of the Great Ones) are the spectators of the ceremony and represent nearly the entire population of the pueblo—as many as four hundred people huddled together in the dim space of the kiva. The men sit in the southeast corner, while the women and children usually sit by themselves on the north side. There are no seats. People sit on the floor on sheepskins or folded blankets. Everyone wears a blanket pulled over his head and shoulders, almost covering his face.

The ritual, of course, is not the drama of an individual or of a god, but rather an expressive group experience—the type of grand tribal saga once understood in the ancient Western world as an epic.

Only Tewa Indians are allowed at the San Juan Rain-Power Ceremony. They alone may witness this tribal drama. The scope of Pueblo ceremonial life is unique. The transformation of a person into a kachina is actually a disciplined living-out of hitherto unlived aspects of the "actor's" personal mentality. In the most findamental sense this process of transformation and the actions that take place following the transformation are an essential, creative experience, both for the performer and for the audience—since that which takes place is *real* in the absolute sense of the word and not simply as a matter of suspended disbelief. To Pueblo performers and their people the experience is similar, perhaps, to dream, as it possesses a sense of unreality, as well as great evocative power—verisimilitude and a persuasive though misty significance.

The Butterfly Dance of San Ildefonso Pueblo, showing the dancers as they emerge from the kiva.

PROLOGUE: THE RESURRECTION OF THE MASKS

THE PROLOGUE to the ceremony begins seven nights before the rain-power drama. On the first night the cacique, his assistants, and the elders of the sponsoring moiety gather to plan the ceremony. In the late evening of the second night the officials of the Winter People visit the houses of the pueblo, calling out each Winter Man. There, in the darkness of the New Mexico desert, they formally invite him to the small kiva.

WAR CAPTAIN

Come to the small kiva tonight, my friend.

Soon all the pueblo Winter Men begin to assemble in the small kiva of the Winter People. Everyone who enters the kiva performs the Feeding Rite, by taking a bit of sacred cornmeal and blowing his breath upon it, then sprinkling it on the ground near the kachina masks (never directly upon them) as he whispers the Feeding Prayer.

WINTER MEN

Partake of this sacred cornmeal, you Rain Powers, So you may have strength in your mysterious bodies.

The Winter Men then repeat the Feeding Rite for the Fire Power Fa'tege'eno. At last, when all the men have arrived, the Winter cacique stands.

WINTER CACIQUE

Children of the female Great Ones, children of the male Great Ones, we gather because a great plan fills our minds. We have decided that, as an offering to the powers, we shall have the Rain-Power Ceremony that we might multiply in children and assure fertility of the soil and abundance of both corn and game.

By repeating what has been said, the assembly of Winter Men assure the cacique that they agree to his plan. Then they silently return to their homes.

On the third night, following the formal announcement in the pueblo of the Rain-Power Ceremony, the Winter Men gather again in the small kiva.

WINTER CACIQUE

Let us now decide who will serve.

He takes the mask of the chief kachina, and a few of the men are tried out—by putting the mask on and performing the movements and sounds characteristic of the particular kachina. Finally one man is chosen.

WINTER CACIQUE

Now let us see how well you can impersonate the other Great Ones.

One by one the kachina masks are donned by the men, who attempt to perform perfectly the movements and sounds of each kachina. The elders thoughtfully make their choice, picking those who will represent the rain powers. The selected men now go to their homes, where they tell their wives of their success.

The Zuni Rain Dance is held frequently during the summer. The final and public part of this elaborate rite of the summer solstice are Rain Dances in which the principal dancers are called the korkokshi, "dancers for good." The dancers are covered with pink clay gathered at the Sacred Lake. The head is adorned with macaw and eagle feathers. The bearded masks are made of buckskin that has been painted blue and are hung with strands of braided horsehair. Spruce garlands are used as anklets and girdles. The kilt is woven by the Hopi and secured from them through trade. The costumed "females" are, of course, male dancers, as women are not allowed to participate. The Zuni sacred clowns, or mudheads, participate in the Rain Dance and are among the most sacred of Zuni kachinas, wearing masks of canvas that suggest the idiot offspring of incestuous unions.

On the fourth night the chosen men take their bedrolls to the kiva. The men who will be kachinas spend the next four nights in the small kiva of the Winter People, where they undergo the Purification Rite. They abstain from meat, salt, and sex. Every morning they go to the fields to feed the Corn Powers with sacred cornmeal while they recite the Morning Prayer. Every night they feed the masks by sprinkling cornmeal on the floor before them. After this nightly feeding of the powers, the masks are taken up and worn while the men practice their roles in the ceremony.

On the fourth and fifth evenings the faces and bodies of those who will become the kachinas are ceremonially painted. Then the Winter cacique passes out holy water. The men take it in their mouths, swallowing some, spit the rest into their hands, and rub it over their bodies saying:

MEN

May it be so. May I have strength. May I continue to be loved and liked and gain good things. May it be so.

PART ONE: THE SACRED CLOWNS

INSIDE THE large kiva small fires burn and many candles flicker. Two guards scrutinize the people to make certain that strangers do not enter the sacred place. One by one the Children of the Great Ones climb down the ladder and silently spread their sheepskins and take seats on the floor. Then the governor of the pueblo and the caciques and priestesses arrive and are seated.

MEN

O rainpowermen; O rainpowerwomen; O rainpowerboys; O rainpowergirls; make your robes from this sacred fog. May we catch up with that for which we are always searching.

Suddenly from above thunder rumbles. It is the clowns, on the top of the kiva, making the sound of thunder with their feet. Everyone laughs as the clowns tumble through a circular hole in the ceiling and lower themselves into the kiva. Excitedly the people sprinkle sacred cornmeal from their right hands in the paths of the clowns. Each clown then sits down and makes stylized movements while peering at the people.

FIRST CLOWN

Hey, Little Twin Brother, what kind of place is this?

SECOND CLOWN

Looks like hell to me—just take a look at all those devil-headed people all around us!

FIRST CLOWN

You are right, Brother. Just get a load of that woman over there . . . she's staring at me.

SECOND CLOWN

Maybe she's got the hots for you.

Everyone laughs as the clowns carefully circle the kiva, peering at the people. The First Clown goes to the side where the men are seated and stares at them. They hide under their blankets, hoping to escape the clown's sarcastic jokes. Meanwhile the Second Clown has been looking over the women.

FIRST CLOWN

Hey, Twin Brother, get a look at this kid over here. I get the feeling that he looks just like you. Hey, maybe he's your little mistake!

The people laugh.

SECOND CLOWN

A-ha, Little-Brother-Older-Than-I, do you believe your eyes? Just look at who is sitting over here! It's none other than the governor! Have you heard the stories about him? They say that he's been making it with the wife of the war captain!

FIRST CLOWN

I don't know about you, Twin Brother, but I'm getting tired of these people. We've come a long way, and maybe it's time to take a rest stop. What do you think?

SECOND CLOWN

You've got a point, Little-Brother-Older-Than-I. Let's take a load off our feet and have some food.

Now the clowns unwrap their sheepskin packs and sit down near the caciques with their supply of meat and bread. They break off small bits of food and throw them to the ground while mumbling the Food-Offering Prayer. Then they eat some of the food.

CLOWNS

Hey, all you dead ones, have something to eat so your bodies get strong.

FIRST CLOWN

Ever notice how people talk when they eat?

SECOND CLOWN

Sure, they do it all the time. How about it, Little-Brother-Older-Than-I, how about talking? Tell me a story!

FIRST CLOWN

Okay . . . let's see. The other day I was just walking along minding my own business when I saw Sweet Grass going out of her home . . . and pretty soon guess who came along to say hello to her?

SECOND CLOWN

I bet it was Bear's Heart!

FIRST CLOWN

You said it, Little-Brother-Older-Than-I! And that's not all he did either!

SECOND CLOWN

And do you have any idea what I saw when I was down by the river last week?

FIRST CLOWN

No, Little-Brother-Older-Than-I, what did you see when you were down by the river last week?

SECOND CLOWN

Well . . . get this! I saw Bosom Plenty being chased by Tall Chief.

FIRST CLOWN

Yeah? Well, tell me, did he get her? And how many times did he get her?

The people laugh as the clowns finish their meal and distribute bits of bread and meat to the people, saying:

CLOWNS

Here, throw this away. Don't eat any of this.

Then they roll their sheepskins, tie them carefully, and place them at the feet of the caciques.

CLOWNS

Excuse me, would you please not take care of this for me.

PART TWO: THE BRINGING OF THE RAIN POWERS

SECOND CLOWN

Hey, Brother, let's cut out this fooling around and get down to business.

Stepping over the women and children seated at his right and walking to one of the fireplaces along the north wall, the First Clown collects a bit of ash and carries it to the center of the kiva.

FIRST CLOWN

Let's try our luck!

He claps his hands, turning the ashes into a little cloud of dust. Then he looks upward and shades his eyes with his hand in a bold pantomimic gesture, as if peering into the distant heavens. He is searching the sky for the rain powers, who move through the air on clouds. This searching gesture with one hand is repeated each time a clown describes what he sees.

FIRST CLOWN

Ah . . . I don't see a thing. Hmmm, tell you what, Little-Brother-Older-Than-I, why don't you give it a try.

SECOND CLOWN

Didn't you just tell me that you couldn't see anything?

FIRST CLOWN

Yes, that's exactly what I said. I didn't see a thing.

Second Clown claps his hands and makes another little ash cloud.

SECOND CLOWN

Ah! . . . I don't see anything either.

The clowns continue their search of the heavens: north, west, south, and east. They toss a bit of ash in one direction but then swing around and look in the wrong direction. Again and again they try to see something, but the result is always the same.

CLOWNS

I don't see anything.

FIRST CLOWN

Hey, Twin Brother, didn't you just tell me that you couldn't see anything?

SECOND CLOWN

That's right. Not a thing!

FIRST CLOWN

Well I've got news for you—I see Thundercloud fondling Good Water.

(Everyone laughs.)

And I can also see something very far away— a lake called the Muddy Water.

SECOND CLOWN

Yes, you're right. I can see the water moving along, churning and bubbling. And I can hear the water splashing.

He mimes the motion of the water and imitates its splashing sounds.

SECOND CLOWN

There's some kind of excitement in the lake, but that's all I can see. Come on, you give it a try and see what you can see!

FIRST CLOWN

Didn't you just tell me that you saw the Muddy Water Lake and that was all? Well, out there I see a head sticking out, one lonely head.

SECOND CLOWN

Didn't you just say that you saw one lonely head sticking out?

FIRST CLOWN

That's right.

SECOND CLOWN

Well, that lonely head is coming out now, and there is another one, too, and it's coming out . . . and another one . . . and another one and another. They just keep coming. And now they're lifting the Cloudflower out of the lake and carrying it in their arms. More of them are coming out, bringing the Cloudflower and the power to make rain . . . the power to raise watermelons, the power to raise muskmelons . . . the power to raise squash, wheat, corn . . . the power to hunt deer, the power to hunt buffalo, the power to hunt rabbits, and the power to kill skunks. Wow!

(Everyone laughs.)

Okay, Little-Brother-Older-Than-I, take a quick look and see what you can see!

FIRST CLOWN

You told me they were coming out of the Muddy Water Lake. Well, let's see . . . now they are rising from the lake and lifting their fog Rainbow and their Cloudflower, rising with their Thunder and Lightning, with bird songs and cricket chirps. And now they are coming to the Stone Man Lake, and there are many more of them in Stone Man Lake and they're coming out too. They just keep coming out.

SECOND CLOWN

Didn't you just tell me that they were coming out of Stone Man Lake? Well, let me tell you this: they're still coming out! There are really a whole bunch of them! They're coming with power to raise corn, muskmelon, and wheat, and with their power to hunt deer and buffalo and rabbit, and with all this power they are moving to Stone Man Mountain, and now

they are right smack on top of Stone Man Mountain! But they don't stop there . . . they're coming to Thunder Lake, and there they go back down under the water again. But wait a minute! They're coming up again with many others! Just take a look at that! There are more and more and more of them . . . coming our way.

FIRST CLOWN

Didn't you just tell me that they were coming closer and closer? Well, I can see them arrive . . . right here in San Juan! They've just gotten to our garbage dump! They are arriving with all their power to bring rain and fertility and . . . and now you go ahead, Little-Brother-Older-Than-I, you tell me what you see!

Three priestesses arise, and each walks slowly in an elongated pattern to the caciques and then to the ladder, performing the Sanctifying Rite by taking cornmeal from their baskets, blowing their breath over it, and then sprinkling it on the floor, making a narrow path for the rain powers, while the clowns continue excitedly reporting on the progress of the rain powers' journey to the pueblo. When the path has reached the ladder, the priestesses return to their seats, lowering to the ground just as the rain powers arrive at the kiva entrance. First clown claps his hands and shades his eyes.

FIRST CLOWN

Didn't you say that they had arrived at our lovely garbage dump?

SECOND CLOWN

That's right.

FIRST CLOWN

Well, from there they are coming along with their Cloudflower, with their Thunder and Lightning, and bringing with them birds singing and crickets chirping; with their power to bring the rain, and fertility, and growth. With all these great goodnesses they are entering our pueblo. Now they are getting closer; I can see them coming into the very center of San Juan, and now . . . and now they are reaching this very spot, the Earth's Navel at the Sacred Stone Shrine . . . yes, they are waiting at Earth's Navel Sacred Stone Shrine laying their fog Rainbow down and depositing their Cloudflower and breathing easy. But now you give it a try, Little-Brother-Older-Than-I.

While the clowns are bringing in the rain powers, the Winter Men, wrapped in blankets, line up near the kiva entrance and gradually turn their backs to the audience and stretch out their arms in such a way that their blankets form a screen concealing the kiva entrance. Behind this screen the assistants lead the masked kachinas from the small kiva, where they have been preparing themselves, into the main kiva. They come silently down the ladder, still unseen by the people, lining up in the shadows behind the blanket screen. Once they have assembled, the assistants take the silencing cornhusks from the resounding belts of the kachinas and give each rain power his yucca whip, melons, rabbits, evergreen tree, and other paraphernalia.

SECOND CLOWN

Didn't you tell me that they had arrived at the Earth's Navel?

FIRST CLOWN

You're absolutely right, Twin Brother, that is what I said.

Second clown claps and lifts his left hand above his eyes.

SECOND CLOWN

Well, I see what you mean—there they are! And they're coming closer and closer! Here they come! Here they come! Here they come to the foot of the ladder . . . bringing Thunder and Wind and bird songs and cricket chirps. They are at the foot of the ladder with all their power to bring rain and growth and abundance, with their power to raise corn and squash and beans and muskmelons, with their power to kill rabbits and deer and buffalo! At the foot of the ladder! Now Little- Brother-Older-Than-I, tell me what you see.

FIRST CLOWN

You said they are at the foot of the ladder, didn't you?

SECOND CLOWN

Yes, I did indeed.

FIRST CLOWN

Well, from the foot of the ladder they start climbing the steps . . . they keep climbing and climbing, climbing and climbing until they are right here on the kiva roof over our heads.

SECOND CLOWN

Here they are with their Thunder, their Wind, their Lightning, their bird calls, their cricket songs!

FIRST CLOWN

Here they are with their power to bring corn, to bring squash, to bring watermelon; with their deer-killing power, their buffalo-killing power, their fox-killing power, their power to bring Rain and Thunder and Lightning, their power to bring fertility and growth and abundance, right here on the kiva above us.

PART THREE: THE SOLEMN ENTRANCE OF THE RAIN POWERS

SUDDENLY A deafening noise is unleashed from behind the blanket screen. Then there is a wild roar from the top of the kiva opening, and the powers appear to drop into the closely packed, dimly lighted kiva, humid with the breathing of huddled people. With the sudden appearance of the powers come their fearsome Thunder, as well as the lovely song of birds, the jingle of hundreds of tiny bells attached to their waists and moving feet. These hoots, whoops, and piercing calls identify each power.

Now a long bony white hand reaches down through the circular opening in the kiva ceiling and tosses corn and piñons to the people, who joyously reach out for them. But the clowns are not happy. They shiver and shake and cry fearfully and rush for their sheepskin rolls, which they have left in the care of the caciques. Quickly they unroll the skins, fasten them around their waists, and, feigning utter fear, they huddle together and tremble. In this manner they stumble toward the entrance to welcome the great ones.

THE CLOWNS

Come, Great Ones, and warm yourselves in our hearts. Yes, yes, Great Ones, come to us and be welcome!

The first power to make his appearance from behind the blanket screen is Chief Rain Power. He stomps his feet. The bells around his waist and ankles resound, and the colored tufts of yarn around his knees surge with his movements. A feathered headdress tops his mask; his large turquoise earrings shine, while in his hands are the threatening yucca whips which all the rain powers carry. Suddenly the squeals and hoots of the other rain powers resound from behind the blanket screen where they are still hidden. Slowly and with great majesty Chief

Rain Power advances on the caciques, preceded by First Clown, who has welcomed him and now leads him forward. First Clown walks backward in front of the rain power and slowly leads him without ever touching him.

FIRST CLOWN

This way, Great One, this way.

The People feed the rain power with cornmeal, on which they exhale their breath and then throw on the path of the kachina.

THE PEOPLE

O Great Ones who come to see us, we are happy that you are here and we give you welcome.

Chief Rain Power gives his watermelon to First Clown, who carries it to the caciques. In the meantime Sun Rain Power has entered. Second Clown welcomes him and leads him to the caciques. First Clown now welcomes Third Rain Power. Gradually eight or ten rain powers are welcomed by the clowns. When all the rain powers have entered, the thunder, wind, and bird sounds end and the blanket screen is folded.

PART FOUR: THE RECEPTION OF THE RAIN POWERS

FIRST CLOWN approaches the rain powers with outstretched arms.

FIRST CLOWN

Yes, Great Ones! Let us be friends!

Chief Rain Power does not respond to this offer but strikes the clown with his whip.

FIRST CLOWN

Ouch, goddamn, that hurts like hell!

He jumps out of the way of the whip and then, cautiously, stretches out his arms once again.

FIRST CLOWN

Aw, come on! Let's be friends!

Chief Rain Power now extends his arms alternately to the right and left in a gesture of welcome. Then each of the other powers, who continually move around the kiva in an elongated circle, offers the clowns a gesture of friendship. Now Chief Rain Power approaches the caciques.

SECOND CLOWN

Ah, O Great One, I believe that you have something on your mind that you'd like to say. Right?

Chief Rain Power nods with his whole body and continues his grunting and stomping. He then points to himself and the other powers, indicating "we," then motions around the kiva—"have come," then points to the place before him—"here," then points from the mouth on his mask toward the caciques to express his wish to talk to them—"We have come here to talk to you." The clowns are jubilant that they have understood Chief Rain Power. They now hurry to a very young man and make him stand up before the rain power. Chief Rain Power shakes his head violently and roars. The young man is obviously not the person with whom the powers wish to talk. So Second Clown motions both caciques to stand. Now Chief Rain Power is pleased and commences to make gestures, which the Winter cacique interprets for the people: "We...have come...from far...as we were concerned...about you...and we wanted...to see...how our Children ...are getting along. It has reached...my ear... that you people...have not listened...to us...and we...have come...to punish you."

WINTER CACIQUE

No, Great Ones, we have not been bad. We have been good people, haven't we, Children of the Great Ones?

PEOPLE

Yes, yes, yes!

WINTER CACIQUE

We are glad that the Great Ones have come to see their Children. But we do not wish to detain you. And we hope you will find your loved ones when you return to them in the place where you dwell.

Now the caciques are seated.

PART FIVE: THE BLESSING BY THE RAIN POWERS

THE MEN RISE and gradually form a line, which, when they stretch out their arms, creates the blanket screen once again. First Clown addresses Chief Rain Power.

FIRST CLOWN

Well, it's been nice seeing you.

SECOND CLOWN

Yeah, it's been great. But this climate is probably far too hot for you here. So you really should be getting back to your own kind. I'm sure your loved ones are already missing you.

The rain powers leave their circular procession around the kiva and one by one disappear behind the blanket screen. Each rain power, before leaving, stops near the exit and performs his Blessing Rite. As solemnly as they entered, the rain powers now disappear. When the last rain power has vanished, the clowns giggle.

FIRST CLOWN

Well, thank goodness for that! They're finally gone, those damn troublemakers!

PART SIX: THE MAN CEREMONY

NOW THE Silent One enters from behind the blanket screen. He stands alone in the dimly lighted kiva, a clownish rain power wearing a humorous mask with a crooked mouth. He is silent. There is total silence in the kiva except for the feet of the Silent One tapping heavily on the floor as he advances, with the slow gait of an old man, carrying a bow and arrow and pausing now and again to shake himself from head to foot. First Clown stares impolitely.

FIRST CLOWN

Hey, who is this guy supposed to be, anyway?

SECOND CLOWN

Maybe he's some kind of old tramp.

FIRST CLOWN

But wait a minute, maybe he's a Great One! Excuse me, mister, could you by any chance be one of our Great Ones?

The Silent One nods emphatically.

SECOND CLOWN

A-huh! I thought so! But tell me, what are you doing, Great One? It looks to me from your movements that you are looking for something.

The Silent One puts his hands with outstretched forefingers to his head, symbolizing "deer."

FIRST CLOWN

A-hah, you are looking for a deer, right!

SECOND CLOWN

And you want to know which way the deer went?

The Silent One gestures: "Which way?"

FIRST CLOWN

That's funny...we didn't see any deer go through here.

SECOND CLOWN

Hmm, tell us, Great One, why are you hunting deer?

The Silent One indicates: "Here are the deer's tracks."

FIRST CLOWN

Hmm, but tell me, Great One, if you find a deer what will you do with it?

The Silent One answers by lifting his bow and arrow.

SECOND CLOWN

A-huh, so that's it! But tell me, Great One, where would you shoot him?

The Silent One points to his heart. Then he continues to explore the kiva with great care.

SECOND CLOWN

But what are you looking for now? You act like you have lost something, Great One.

The Silent One shakes his head.

FIRST CLOWN

Hmm, seems to me you have something on your mind, Great One.

The Silent One nods.

SECOND CLOWN

But tell me, what is it that you have on your mind, Great One?

The Silent One holds both hands before his chest in a gesture indicating small, firm breasts.

FIRST CLOWN

Ah yes!

Searching among the people, he spots a handsome young boy and asks him to stand up.

FIRST CLOWN

How about this! Is this what you want?

The people laugh, and the Silent One exasperatedly shakes his head.

SECOND CLOWN

Sweet Meats, where are you?

In answer to the call, a young girl, clad in a shawl and mantle, comes forward and stands silently in front of the two clowns.

FIRST CLOWN

So this is what you want! Well, tell me, Great One, what are you going to give her?

The Silent One unties a freshly killed rabbit from his waist and gives it to the clown, who passes it on to the girl. Sweet Meats accepts the evergreen bundle containing the rabbit and holds it in front of her with slightly bent arms. Second Clown asks Sweet Meats for her shawl. She takes off her shawl and then stands motionlessly in front of the Silent One. But he is not pleased and gestures that she should lie down. First Clown arranges the girl's shawl on the floor directly in front of her in the shape of a woman's body lying prone for her lover.

FIRST CLOWN

All right, she is willing. Go ahead.

The Silent One shakes his head and gestures that she should spread her legs. The people laugh. Second Clown stretches the ends of the shawl that represent the girl's legs, but again the Silent One indicates that the legs should be spread even wider. The clown complies as the people laugh again. Then the Silent One puts down his bow and arrow and enacts the Blessing Rite. He reaches out with his hands into space to catch the breath and goodness from the air. He catches the goodness from above; he catches the goodness from below; he catches the goodness from the north, the west, the south, and the east. He passes his hands over his body, as if trying to get the goodness and strength from within himself; then he takes all this goodness and strength and, by clapping his hands, he sends all of it to the girl, who stands silent and a bit embarrassed.

FIRST CLOWN

Looks like he's already finished.

SECOND CLOWN

Well, how was it, Sweet Meats? Did it hurt?

The people laugh.

FIRST CLOWN

Now, Great One, you have done the Man Ceremony.

(*Ser poer p'a* means both "man ceremony" and "sexual intercourse," so the people laugh.)
With this the Silent One disappears behind the blanket screen. The clowns now provide outrageous imitations of the rain powers, gesturing and roaring ridiculously, to the people's delight. Then the clowns pick up the sacred melons the rain powers brought with them. They break the melons into small pieces, which they distribute to the people, who eat the blessed melon while the old women throw bits of the melon to the ground, to feed the dead. Both clowns roll their sheepskins, sliding them over their shoulders, and, giving the Blessing Rite to everyone, they disappear behind the blanket screen. Then the men forming the screen slowly fold their blankets.

PART SEVEN: THE THANKSGIVING

THE TWO CACIQUES stand and speak.

SUMMER CACIQUE

It is true that we have been evil, but the Great Ones with supreme goodness have been generous. They came to punish us, but instead they granted favors. Now this night made sacred by the Great Ones being among us should remind us to give kindness and helpfulness to each other and to bring peace and harmony equal to the greatness of Children of the Great Ones. We have come here in the hope for life and with the hope of being loved and liked and to receive goodness from the powers. We have become tired, but tiredness and soreness are not all that have come to us.

THE PEOPLE

Yes, we have worked hard, and we have become tired and our bodies have grown sore. But we have done this in order that we might have children and that we might be loved and liked and achieve our hopes on the path we live.

WINTER CACIQUE

Growing tired in our bodies, but more than tiredness and soreness have come to us, for now we have won a life of good things.

The cacique gives his blessing by bringing the goodness from himself and throwing it to the people with both open hands. The people catch the goodness and take deep breaths to take in the great goodness bestowed upon them.

THE PEOPLE

We pray to go on being loved and liked and taking in the Goodness of the Mother of Us All and catching up with what has always drawn us to win a life of all good things we wish for.

WINTER CACIQUE

It is open! Now go to your homes without worry, without weeping, without sadness.

THE PEOPLE

May it be so.

RELIGION INTO RITUAL

S ONG AND DANCE are intrinsic to religion among Indians. Words—chanted, sung, or spoken—are valued by an Indian primarily for the reaction they produce within himself rather than for any effect they might have on others. The first stage of Indian ritual is almost always the rise of the singer on his own song to a plane of power—a place of contact with the forces that move the universe. In many tribes this power is obtained by reciting words or sounds four times, four often being a sacred number. The words and sounds are only the small visible aspect of a far greater mystery, which lies beneath speech. For this reason the nature of Indian songs requires the comprehension of a larger context, even among the people for whom they are originally intended. Ritual words are for the Indian singer only an intimation, a complex abbreviation of a larger idea, a sound or a word or two that conveys something wider and truer than what is actually spoken. As an old holy man observed, "You sometimes see an Indian singing and crying while he sings. It isn't what he is singing that makes him cry; it is what the song makes him remember. That is what he is crying about." A whole cycle of tribal or individual experience can lie behind a song's simple articulate phrasing, like this brief song from the Teton Dakota, which was recorded by ethnologist and musicologist Frances Densmore:

> *Soldiers,*
>   *You fled.*
> *Even the eagle dies.*

In the north, among the tribes of what is now the United States and Canada, theocracy and massive temples were not usually the basis of the spiritual life of the people. Certain influences toward monumentality and spiritual dictatorship came northward from Central Mexico and made an impact on the social organizations there. But instead of evolving and dominating North America, these societies had their brief triumph and rather mysteriously declined and vanished prior to the arrival of the white invaders. Though there are vestiges of various Muskogean peoples (generally referred to as the Natchez culture), who once numbered well over 50,000 in Georgia, Mississippi, and parts of Louisiana and Tennessee, precious little was found in 1492 of their once-great Natchez world. The complexity of the Natchez chiefdom was reminiscent of the Aztec realm; their chief was known as the Great Sun, and the hereditary nobles were called Suns. The chiefdom was a pure theocracy and the religious practices were the most inhumane in North America, involving human sacrifice and the ritual burning of infants. Though the tribes of North America had their own forms of inhumanity, none of their practices was nearly so intent upon cruelty and social inequity as those of the Natchez and some of the tribes south of the Rio Grande River. Quite to the contrary, the social and religious practices of the northern peoples were astonishingly removed from many of the characteristic brutalities and exploitations that have marked other societies, a fact noted by the artist-explorer George Catlin when he praised the Indian: "I love a people who are honest

without laws, who have no jails and no poorhouses. I love a people who keep the commandments without ever having read them or heard them preached from the pulpit."

There is a popular notion that the Indians of North America possessed a religious viewpoint consisting entirely of belief in a Great Spirit. Such ideas were fabricated by whites who had early contact with Indians and were unable to see them for what they were. These white men projected their own values on social organizations for which such values were entirely inappropriate. Among the tribes of North America there is a pantheistic belief in a primal world force and its embodiment in all the elements. This power or energy exists in all things and beings in the universe. But it varies greatly in degree, and therefore different ceremonies, songs, and rites are required to maintain a tribe's harmony with this awesome power, which is the basis of everything that exists. The concept of power is expressed variously as *orenda* (Iroquois), *wakanda* (Dakota), *manito* (Algonquian), *pokunt* (Shoshone), and *coen* (Athapaskan).

Indians are largely innocent of all the categories into which the universe has been divided by white people seeking one truth, and they are inclined to speak of a marvelously performed ceremony with its richness of songs and its complex music not as art but as the sacred transactions of nature. They refer to the achievement of the ceremony not as something beautiful but rather as something good—but in the sensual and not the moral meaning of that word. Indians are wonderfully remote from Western artistic self-consciousness. In the white world the arts are conceptually separate. People have come to think of both the practice and enjoyment of art as

Within the sacred chamber: a rare photograph of the Lallaconte Kiva at Walpi Pueblo, Arizona, where a young Hopi girl guards the small entrance through which women and children have access to the chamber (the men enter from a laddered hole in the ceiling). The murals depict lightning, a raincloud, the Thunderbird, a corn plant, and a Hano clown. The paintings predate the whitewash that was applied around the outline of the iconography. (1901)

private efforts. But in Indian society privacy is not necessarily a virtue; the arts are simply aspects of public life which bring together dancing, poetry, and music into a single function: ritual as the all-embracing expressive act. As for the dancer, the singer, or the musician, they simply don't exist; the "artist" is a non-Indian creation. White people look upon the artist as distinct from the artisan. Even the most hostile critic wouldn't call sculptor Henry Moore a stonemason, Louise Nevelson a carpenter, or Mexican muralist Diego Rivera a house painter. For Indians before Columbus this distinction of artist as opposed to artisan did not exist. Indians would have seen no more reason to put pottery or painting in a museum than in a well-planted field of corn. Part of this Indian nonchalance about art comes no doubt from their unlimited number of gifted singers, dancers, musicians, and makers of art objects—a prevalence not so remarkable when the nearly universal artistic ability of Indians is understood as a form of aesthetic literacy. At an age when most American and European children are starting to use a pencil to learn to write, Indian children are probably learning to dance, to make music or pottery, to carve with a knife, or to express themselves through tribal iconography and the elaborate oral tradition of their people. This pervasive artistic facility is often discovered in societies in which writing does not exist and in which traditional values are handed down orally. Dance and the other arts have always been aspects of the tradition of Indians. But as an individual effort and as something with universal significance, the idea of art emerged slowly, and only in recent decades has it become self-contained and authored by an individual. For Indians, "art" is still an organic process rather than an end product. Indian tribal life is so unified that there is simply no need for art to *communicate* anything—it is only when the uniformity of social values in a society begins to shatter that meaning in the arts comes into existence. But for Indians art is valued for its magical power, and hence there is a mystical basis for aesthetic judgment among Indians.

When people unfamiliar with Indian customs first encounter native ceremonies, they are inclined to be swept away by the sheer exoticism of the performers—and the lavish embellishment of every aspect of the ritual acts and paraphernalia. But nothing in a ceremony is purely decorative. Nothing is ever quite what it appears to be to those outside a culture. Conventional artistic values are not easily applied to something as vast in time and space and involving so large an isolated population as the material culture created autonomously in North America. An object of art created by an Indian—whether a costume or a piece of pottery—is seen by the outsider to be elaborately covered with designs. But such objects are not decorated in the same way that a European teacup, for instance, is decorated with painted roses in order, presumably, to distract from the fact that it is in reality a teacup. There are people who will insist that the roses on the teacup are symbolic and ceremonial, but such decoration seems to have a great deal more to do with etiquette than with ritual.

The Redheaded Woodpecker Dance (Jump Dance) was performed by Indians of Weitchpec, California, in the years between performances of the White Deers Dance. Their headdresses are made of feathers from the redheaded woodpecker, necklaces are of dentalium shell money, loin robes of white deerskin, and their rattles were woven from grasses. (ca. 1896)

When the Indian potter collects clay, she asks the consent of the riverbed, and she sings its praises for having made something as beautiful and as useful as clay. And when the potter fashions the clay into a form, she does so by emulating the shapes of sacred things in which there is power and in which there is life. And when she fires her pottery, to this day she still offers prayers so the fire won't discolor or burst her wares. And, at last, when she paints her pottery, she imprints it with the images that give it life and power—because to an Indian pottery is something "significant" and not just a utility but a "being" for which there is as much a natural order as there is for things that are persons or foxes or trees.

Performed during the winter, the Shalako, or House-Blessing Ceremony, of the Zuni people is a forty-nine-day ritual enactment of the Zuni emergence and migration history, as well as a prayer for propagation and tribal well-being. The dead return during the ceremony and are honored and fed. A ten-month period is needed for the preparation rites of the ceremony: the houses which will honor the shalakos are built or renovated extensively. There are eight such houses, six for the shalakos, one for Sayatasha and the Council of Powers (called the Long Horn House) and one for the koyemshi (mudheads). The shalakos are giant couriers of the Rain Makers, one to represent each of the six kivas. The Sayatasha—Rain Power of the North, or Long Horn—supervises all activities preceding the appearance of the shalakos. Hututu—Rain Power of the South—also participates as deputy of Sayatasha. Here the towering shalakos cross the special causeway constructed for them to get to the south bank of the river. (1896)

The arts are a central and inclusive aspect of the religions of Indians. Everything in the life of the tribes has a ritual unified and pervasive cosmological significance. This religious integrity not only includes the unique costumes, painted imagery, and pottery of Indians but also provides geographical places and structures with a complex sacred connotation. The house-building and blessing ceremonies of the Zuni Indians of New Mexico are examples of the interface between daily life and sacred life.

The Zuni Shalako ends with the going out of the powers at noon. The final ceremony is held on the south side of the causeway where the dancers place prayer plumes in holes dug in the ground. Six plumes are placed at each end of the runway where the shalakos have performed their curiously elegant smooth-running motions. Then the powers depart, passing long lines of Zuni people who sprinkle cornmeal on them.

The Yaqui Easter Festival

THE YAQUI SETTLEMENTS of southern Arizona conduct their most complex ceremonies during Lent. The impact that the missionaries had among these Mexican people living just within the border of the United States was thorough—so thorough that their major ceremony is a primal version of the Catholic liturgy for the Lenten season and Easter—a play that interlaces many elaborate elements of both Catholic and Yaqui rites. The basic theme of the Yaqui Easter ceremonies is also borrowed from Christianity: the triumph of good over evil. Like most Indian rites the two opposing factions are organized as societies which impersonate the polemic principals of their ritual theme.

Judas, bristling with weapons and symbols of evil, is the saint of the chapayekas.

The members of the Fariseo (Pharisee) Society represent the enemies of Christ. The evil chapayekas, the soldiers of the Fariseos, are dressed in sinister masks of painted hide or paper and carry swords and daggers of wood.

In order to prevent Judas' evil from entering the hearts of the impersonators, each chapayeka carries the cross of his rosary in his mouth when he is wearing the mask of the evil ones.

The members of the Matachina Society, a men's dance group under vow to Mary, are called soldiers of the Virgin. They are the allies of the church group during the Easter ceremonies. Here they dance with rattles before the cross. They wear headdresses of paper flowers and ribbons and carry wands decorated with bright feathers. The boys wear white garments and serve as the guardians of the Virgin.

The church group is led by the maestros, who are opposite forces of the chapayekas. Though not ordained these good spirits perform the special services in Spanish and Latin that are unique to the Yaqui Easter rites.

The pivotal struggle of the ceremonies is the attack upon the church by the forces of evil. The black-clad Fariseos and their masked soldiers march on the church.

The Matachinas and their maestros stand guard before the church, ready to repel any attack.

The evil ones retreat before the Gloria.

Yet another march on the church by the forces of evil.

The church bells ring out the Gloria! On Holy Saturday the Matachinas beat back the Fariseos with a bombardment of flowers, leaves, and confetti. Several of the chapayekas are "killed."

In a triumphant celebration a large effigy of Judas is burned. The chapayekas throw their masks and swords into the fire.

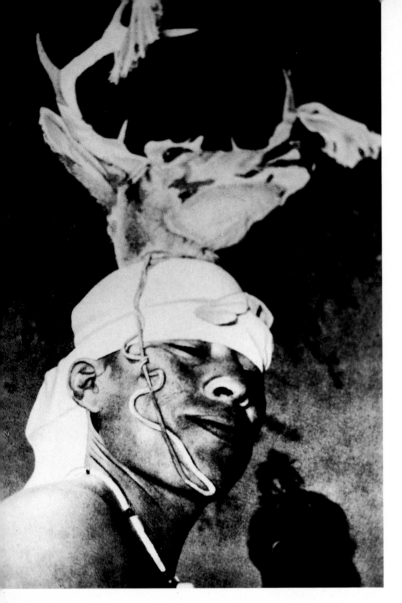

A second group of dancers, the masos, or deer dancers, have their origin in hunting rites but have now been integrated into the Yaqui Easter festival. The most celebrated deer dancers are from the large Yaqui settlements in Mexico. Their elaborate headdresses are composed of real or imitation deer heads fastened to a white cloth on the dancer's head. Red ribbons wound around the deer horns represent flowers.

In addition to the dramatic characters, there is a group of dancers, called the pascolas ("old men of the fiesta") and their three musicians. The pascolas help the Matachinas destroy the Fariseos on Holy Saturday. They wear wooden masks that are painted black with white designs and adorned with long, coarse white hair. Originally the pascolas had the grotesque and humorous qualities of the sacred clowns. Their origin predates the Yaqui Easter festival, but they have been integrated into the Christian ceremonies and their ribald nature has been sanctioned. Here the pascolas (below left), perform while one of their musicians plays the drum and flute simultaneously.

The deer dancers are ritually feared by the Fariseos because they are on the side of the church. Below a pascola and a deer dancer dance to the music at a fiesta on the night before Palm Sunday. The deer dancer sings "deer songs," which are filled with lyrics about flowers and the defeat of the Fariseos at the Gloria.

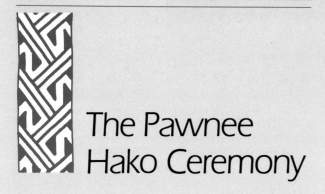

The Pawnee Hako Ceremony

TWO GROUPS ARE necessary for the performance of the Hako Ceremony.[8] One group, the Fathers, initiates the ceremony and pays a ritual visit on the second group, the Children. These two groups cannot belong to the same clan of the tribe, and very often they are members of completely different tribes at considerable distance from each other.

In the old days the leader of the Fathers was usually a chief. Since 1900 he has more often been a man prominent in the tribe, with a large following of relatives who can contribute to the store of articles required for the rites. The Fathers may range in size anywhere from ten to one hundred people. The group includes two holy men who have knowledge of healing with herbs, as well as singers and a kura'hus, or priest.

The original purpose of the ceremony was probably the desire for offspring. Later it changed to a ritual designed to ensure peace and friendship between different clans or tribes. The ritual exchange of gifts is central to the ceremony, as is the use of the peace pipe, so closely associated with the breath-of-life. The term *hako* is not the true name of the ceremony but actually a comprehensive term referring to the various articles that are part of the ritual. Decorated peace pipes—or more correctly, peace pipe stems—feature prominently in the ceremony.

The Hako Ceremony has no fixed time; it is not connected with planting or harvesting, hunting or war, or any other tribal festival. However, it is usually celebrated sometime in the spring, when birds are mating, or in the summer, when birds are nesting and caring for their young, or in the fall, when the birds are flocking—but not in the winter, when many things are asleep. "With the Hako," a Pawnee holy man explained, "we are praying for the gift of life, of strength, of plenty, and of peace. We must make these prayers when life is stirring everywhere."

The general form of the Hako Ceremony is simple despite the interplay of events and songs that elaborate the event. The preliminary rites take place at the lodge of the leader of the Fathers. Then the Fathers set out on their journey to the village of the Children. The large party of the Fathers is impressive as it sets off on foot across the prairie to visit the neighboring group. At the head walks the priest, carrying Mother Corn wrapped in a wildcat skin. At his side walk the Father and the Hako holy men with their assistants, carrying the two "breathing tubes of wood," the pipe stems which have been decorated as part of the preparatory rites of the ceremony. The pipes are embellished from one end to the other with symbolic feathers and paint. Behind the holy men walk two priests with eagle wings to sweep away evil from the path of the party. Then come many singers with their drums. Finally the men, women, and children of the Father's extended family follow the procession, leading ponies loaded with gifts and food supplies.

The procession plods over the prairie, stopping to contemplate and to sing praises for every feature of the land. As the group moves along, the priest appeals constantly to Mother Corn to send them on the right road, an act she alone can accomplish because Tira'wa, the All-Power, has given her authority to lead the Fathers on their journey.

The Children, the people of the host village, have of course been notified that they are to receive the Hako party, and so they are well prepared for their guests. When the Fathers arrive, the pipe is ceremonially smoked, and there are several reciprocal feasts. The visitors sanctify the lodge in which they will stay with imposing processionals and with singing and the waving of eagle feathers.

The central event of the Hako Ceremony is

[8]Major source: Alice Fletcher, *The Hako: A Pawnee Ceremony*, 1900-1901.

the adoption rite. The major figure is not the leader of the Children's village but a specific young person (usually the son of the Children's leader). The child, or Son as he is now called, is given sacred objects used in the Hako including the painted ear of corn representing Mother Corn. The tip is blue, symbolizing the sky; four blue lines running halfway down the ear symbolize the four paths along which the spirits descend to minister to humanity.

The climax of the Hako Ceremony is the uniting of the Father of the visiting group and the Son of the host group, merging old with new. The Hako Ceremony is a prayer for children, that the tribes may increase and be strong, that the people may live long and happily and in peace.

PRELIMINARY RITES

IN THE HAKO CEREMONY one of the most important preliminary rites is the painting of Mother Corn. The priest mixes blue clay in a wooden bowl with water taken from a running stream, and paints an ear of white corn while he sings. This symbolizes the journey of Mother Corn from earth to the place where the All-Power resides. Having arrived there, she is sanctified and returns to the earth to lead the procession that is to bring peace, unity, and plenty to the people.

> We now take blue paint which is the emblem
> of the open sky
> Where the powers live who bring us good
> gifts of life and plenty.
> Then we take green paint which is like Mother
> Earth,
> And we ask from the great sky bountiful
> blessings for Mother Earth.

Then the priest paints the pipe stems while the people sing. They ask that life be given to the stem, which symbolizes the place where Tira'wa lives in the sky. The priest paints the groove red because the passageway by which a man's breath comes and goes to give him life is red.

The singers calls on Kawas, the brown eagle. This great bird has been made by Tira'wa, All-Powerful, and its feathers are tied upon the pipe stem.

> O, Kawas, come with wings outspread in the
> bright sky!
> O, Kawas, come and give new life to all of us!

The people then entreat Tira'wa.

> Tira'wa, listen! You who are so powerful
> above us in the vast silent sky!
> Listen! She stands before you. Mother Corn,
> standing green before you.
> Mother Corn is made the leader that we may
> follow her on our journey.

Mother Corn reaches the blue dome of the world where Tira'wa dwells. Now, having been given *tawitshpa*—the authority to lead in the Hako Ceremony—she descends to Earth by the four paths.

FINDING THE SON

MOTHER CORN leads the spirit of the people in search of the Son. The people's spirits approach the village where the Son lives. But the Son does not see them as they stand before him, for he is sleeping. The people fix their minds upon Mother Corn and upon the Son, thinking of the gifts they will bring to him when they come to him with the Hako. And they think of the gifts that the birds and the animals which attend the sacred objects of the ceremony will bestow upon the Son—long life, children, and plenty. Now the spirit of Mother Corn touches the Son. If the people are earnest, he will respond to her touch. He will not awaken and he will not see her, but he will see in a dream one of the birds which attend the Hako, and he may hear the bird call to him. When he awakens, he will remember his dream and he will know that he has been chosen to be the Son.

> Mother Corn, listen to us! We can see where
> the children live as we approach their
> village!
> Mother Corn, listen to us! We find the Son's
> lodge and pass through the door.
> He lies sleeping, not knowing we are before
> him. Mother Corn, listen!
> Now at her touch comes a dream to him and
> then a bird which calls, "My son!"
> While all along his spirit sleeps. Mother
> Corn, listen!

SENDING THE MESSENGERS

FOUR MESSENGERS are selected by the Father from among his relatives.

> I tell you to travel over the land to the Son,
> And take with you these words of mine and
> give them to him:
> "Listen to what I say! Your Father comes to
> you in haste."

When the messengers arrive at the lodge of the Son, he sends for his family. If, after talking to his kin, he accepts the tobacco offered by the messengers, he must then tell them to return to the Father and to say, "I am ready."

THE SACRED OBJECTS

The people look toward the north, the moon, the night, the mother of the day. To all the Powers of the east, west, south, and north they sing and present themselves. They walk and trace upon the earth the figure of a man: its feet are one with their feet and will move with them as they take four steps, bearing the sacred objects, in the presence of all the Powers. And so they begin their journey to the land of the Son.

> Look down, West Powers, look down upon us!
>   We gaze into the distance where you dwell.
> Thunder and Lightning that bring life, that
>   bring death, look upon us!
> Look down, South Powers, look down upon
>   us! We gaze into the distance where you
>   dwell.
> Daylight and Sunshine, look upon us!
> Look down, North Powers, look down upon
>   us! We gaze into the distance where you
>   dwell.
> Darkness and Moonlight, look upon us!
> Look at us as we lift these sacred things up to
>   you!

MOTHER CORN ASCENDS TO POWER

> The mother leads and we follow,
> Her winding path lies before us.
> She leads us as our fathers were led
> Down through long ages.

The people think of the way, through the Hako, they can make a man who is not their blood a Son; a way that has come down to them from their ancestors like a winding path. This journey the people take is for a sacred purpose, and as they are led by the power in the Mother Corn, they must address with song every object they meet because Tira'wa is in everything. When finally the village of the Children is in sight, the people sing:

> We have come to this place, bringing the Son
>   our gifts.
> Now we see him where he sleeps.
> He is the Son we have sought.

Before, when the Son accepted the gift of tobacco and sent the messengers back to the Hako party, he entered with his closest relatives the lodge set apart for the ceremony. There he has awaited the coming of the Fathers. He seated himself at the south side of the lodge near the door. This place is very humble, and the Son takes it to show that he is not seeking his own honor.

> The Mother Corn, with living breath,
> Now enters into the Son's lodge.
> The Mother Corn, with living breath,
> Now circles within the lodge,
> Walking around within;
> With the breath-of-life walks Mother Corn.

The lodge having been made ready as a nest within which new life can be given and made safe, the Father now performs his first act of recognition and care. He puts new garments on the Son. The garments are very beautiful and fine, rich with embroidery. Then the Son is told to make an offering of smoke to Tira'wa.

> See the smoke billow!
> Rising high, following where his great voice
> Goes, intent to reach the place
> Where the Powers dwell in the vast silent sky.
> See the smoke billow!

Now the criers summon the people to the lodge. They come, dressed in their best attire, and they bring gifts. The feathered pipe stems are brought. They are like the eagle, and the holy place where the stems are placed represents the eagle's nest. A nest is made for the young, and this making of the nest in the lodge of the Son by Kawas (the eagle) fulfills the promise of the Fathers to the Son, as well as the making of a close and good bond, like that of father and son.

When the sun has set and it is dark and the stars are shining in the night, the Children gather in the lodge. After everyone has been seated, wood is piled upon the fire, and when the flames rise high, the kura'hus rises. Then his assistant and the chief also rise, and the Hako (sacred paraphernalia) is taken up. The singers carry the drum and follow the Hako bearers as they move slowly around the lodge and sing.

> Magic visions! Come, we urge you, come into
>   us!
> Bring with you happiness!
> Come, to us, great visions!

The people sing about the visions which the birds on the feathered pipe stems are to bring to the Children. Visions come from the sky, sent by Tira'wa. The people receive great help through visions. Visions can come most readily at night, for Powers travel better at that time. The Fathers call upon the visions and urge them to come to their Children. The visions have heard the call of the Powers of the birds upon the feathered pipe stems, and they begin to descend by the east from their dwelling place in the sky and are coming down toward the lodge. The people sing:

They are coming!

The Children join in the song as the people pass among them the feathered pipe stems. The visions that attend the Hako are now touching the Children, touching them here and there—by their touch giving dreams that will bring the Children health, strength, happiness, and all good things. As the people sing, the visions walk away, for they have done what they came to do. They are now leaving the lodge, and soon the space where they had been is empty. The people pause and think of the visions going away over the silent earth and ascending to their dwelling place.

Magic visions!
They are ascending into the sky to their dwelling
Where they linger above us.

CHANT TO THE SUN

AS THE NIGHT ends, the kura'hus orders the server to lift the skins that hang at the doors of the long passageway of the lodge and to go outside and there to watch for the first glimmer of light. When at last it is dawn, the server comes to announce the new day, and the people rise and take up the Hako implements. They stand in the west, behind the holy place in the lodge, and there, looking toward the east, they sing:

Awake, O Mother, from slumber!
In the east comes dawn where all new life begins.

Mother Earth hears the song. She moves. She awakens. She rises. The leaves and the grass stir; all things move with the breath of the new day. Everywhere life is renewed. This is a very mysterious moment. The people whisper, for they are singing of something very sacred, even though it happens every day.

The Mother awakens from sleep;
She rises, for the night is over;
And the dawn comes
In the east where comes new life.

The people shout:

Daylight has come! Day is here!

The light covers the earth. As the people look through the door of the lodge they can see the trees, and all things in the world stand clearly in the new light. On this, the second day of the Hako, the people remember their father the Sun.

Now see, the ray of our father Sun come upon us.
It comes over all the land, passing into the lodge to touch us and to give us strength.
Was it in dreams that the Fathers saw
Clearly the Hako, with which I now make you my Son?
Was it in dreams they learned how to make you
My own offspring?
Now this we know in truth: the
Dreams come to us when the night is over us;
True it is that he did see them;
In a vision he saw Katasha, where they live.

THE FLOCKING OF THE BIRDS

IN THE SPRING the birds lay their eggs and in the summer they raise their young; in the fall, when all the birds are grown, the nests are deserted and the flocks fly high over the land. In this song which is sung toward the end of the ceremony the people are thinking of the promise of the Hako, that children will be granted to the people, so that they may be many and strong and their flocks will be great.

People gather together like flocking birds,
Circling and coming from many directions.
Their wings make great noise as they move,
As they come together, hurrying into the sky.
They hasten toward the lodge where the Son awaits,
Bringing gifts as they joyfully shout.
Listen! They scream like the great eagle,
Happy in their hearts, as when the bird sees her nest.

The Son selected for the ceremony receives the promises which Mother Corn and Kawas bring—the promise of children, of increase, of long life, of plenty and of peace.

With the day I seek the child,
Among the Children I go seeking
The one the Powers will make
My offspring, my own child.

The ear of corn represents Mother Earth, and the blue paint with which the corn is painted represents the power to bring forth plenty. The people hold the painted ear of corn toward the Son so that the Powers from above and from below may come near.

> *Now we look on the child who is here;*
> *He is the Son we have sought;*
> *He brings us again greetings of the Son:*
> *"Father, come to me, here I sit*
> *Awaiting you here."*

While the people sing, the kura'hus touches the Son on the forehead with the ear of corn. The spirit of Mother Corn, with the power of Mother Earth, touches the child. The touch means the promise of fruitfulness to the child and his people.

The child, surrounded by great forces of creation, is urged by the people to move, to rise and slowly walk as the singing begins. The four steps taken by the child represent the progress of his life.

> *I am ready; come to me now, fearing nothing;*
> *come now to me here.*
> *Stepping forward is the child, he steps with*
> *four steps and enters new life.*

Fresh water taken from a stream is put into a bowl. (The water was collected the previous night, for night is the mother of day; running water means the continuity of life, one generation following another; the bowl that holds the water is like the dome of the sky, the place of Powers that give life.) The child is touched with the water upon the head and the face, an outline is made, which afterward is to become distinct and visible. This first anointment with water is to cleanse and to give strength.

> *Look, my child! Water now has brought to*
> *you the gift of strength.*

The people think of Tira'wa, the All-Power above, as everything everywhere, as the pulse and power that has arranged and thrown down from above everything needed to make a world. What Tira'wa is like, no one knows for no one has been there.

As the people sing, the old man makes the same lines upon the face of the child as he made with the water, singing:

> *Look, my child. Look! Sacred ointment is now*
> *here upon your face.*

The grass from the brush used to paint the Son is made and gathered during a ceremony belonging to the Rain shrine. It represents Toharu, the living covering of Mother Earth. This power, represented by the brush of grass, is now standing before the child. While the people sing, the old man touches the forehead of the child with the brush of grass. The power of Toharu has reached the child, has touched the child and given the strength that comes

> *Look, my child. Look! Grass now waits to*
> *bring to you gifts of food.*

Now the child is painted with pigment representing the red clouds of the dawn, the coming of the new day, the rising sun, and the vigor of life. The power of the new day is now standing before the child. As the people sing, the old man touches the forehead of the child with red paint. The vigor of life touches the child.

> *Look, my child. Look! Red paint waits to*
> *bring to you the vigor of life.*

Now the eagle down is put on. It represents the high, light clouds in the blue sky that are near the place of Tira'wa. It also represents the breath-of-life of the white eagle, the father of the child. While the people sing, the old man opens his hand and lets the down fall upon the child's hair. The soft white clouds near the place of Tira'wa have come down and have covered the head of the child.

> *Look, my child. Look! Down of the eagle*
> *waits with the sign of clouds.*

While the people sing, the old man ties the downy feather to the child's hair. Tira'wa is now with the child as the feather waves over his head.

> *Look, my child! Look! It is the sign that the*
> *Father sends.*

Now the people sing that all is accomplished. The child has been fully prepared, the sacred symbols have been put upon the child, the powers from above have come down, and Tira'wa now breathes over the child, who is told to look into the bowl of water and to behold his face. The child looks into the water and sees his own likeness, as he will see his likeness in his children and his children's children. The face of Tira'wa is also there, giving promise that the life of the child shall go on, as the waters flow over the land.

MAKING THE NEST

A CIRCLE REPRESENTING a nest is drawn by the toe of the holy man because the eagle builds its nest with its claws. The people think of Tira'wa making the world. Therefore the circle represents not only the nest but also the circle of Tira'wa, which was made as the place for people to live. The circle also stands for the kinship groups, the clans, and the tribes. The child represents the young generation and the continuation of life, and when the child is put in the circle, it is like the bird laying its eggs.

> *Within the nest the child rests,*
> *Awaiting the gift sent by the powers,*
> *Descending upon him comes the promise of*
> *life.*

THANKSGIVING

AN OFFERING of sweet smoke is made to Tira'wa, then all traces of the nest are obliterated, and the lodge is once more thrown open to all the people. The children are called. The ponies presented to the Fathers are brought forward by children so that the child of the ceremony may see them. This is now the bond between the two groups of the ceremony, the Fathers and the Children. Then the kura'hus stands and prays with all his spirit that Tira'wa will let the Son grow up and become strong and find favor in his life. This is a very solemn act because the people believe that Tira'wa, although not seen, sends down his breath as they call on him to come to them. As the kura'hus sings this song, he cannot help shedding tears, for he is looking down upon the Son and praying for him deep in his heart. What he says with his song is hidden in its meaning, but it means that the ceremony is a prayer to call down the breath of Tira'wa to give the Son long life and strength and to teach him that he belongs to Tira'wa—that he is the child of Tira'wa and not of his father on earth.

> *Breathe on him!*
> *Breathe on him!*
> *Life you alone can give to him.*
> *Long life, we pray, our Father, give this child life!*
> *Give this child life that we may live!*

The Papago Wine and Rain-Making Ceremony

IN MIDSUMMER, when the Arizona desert is scorched and the sun hangs in a blazing white sky, the Papago Indians camp in the Saguaro National Monument among the unique, towering giants with spiny arms that often reach fifty feet. The Papago families have come to harvest the crimson cactus fruit from which they make jam, candy, syrup and—for a summer rain ritual—a sacred wine.

Once I did not know how to make the liquor.
At the foot of a tree, I lay motionless.
The wind blew.
Dust blew along the dry ground
And cast itself into my face.
Then kinsmen gave me from the bottom of a
*   jar*
The liquid which fermented for me.
Within the liquid I came to my sacred house
And I saw all kinds of winds there lay,
And I saw all kinds of seeds there lay.
Seated upon them was One who powerfully
*   touched me.*
He blew out his winds and his cold.
He pressed against me
And left me moistened and healed.
Then came the growing things.
Then came the delightful evenings
And the delightful dawns.
So hurry, and in any way you can,
Come and swallow my fermented liquor.

When Grandmother, the matriarch, makes the sign the family gets up and is on its way at daybreak, wandering among the great saguaros. The pickers use their kuibits, long picking poles, to pry the red fruit from the cactus.

The cactus fruit is then squeezed from the pods and laid on the ground with the bright red fruit toward the sky, a ritual to please the gods. The harvest is collected in baskets and with the filled baskets on their heads and kuibits in hand, they make the walk back to camp.

Grandmother is responsible for the traditional steps of this old ritual harvest. Over a hot mesquite fire a mixture of fruit and water is boiled.

A gourd utensil is used to ladle the liquid into a loosely woven basket on top of a large pot called an olla, a process that strains the pulp and permits the liquid to collect. The liquid is returned to the fire and slowly cooked into a thick syrup.

The syrup is poured into small ollas, covered with pieces of deer hide stretched over the mouth, tied down, and sealed with a mud paste that dries to the hardness of pottery. While the women complete this work, the men keep the fires burning with wood collected in the desert.

The Papago roundhouse, a ceremonial structure often built next to a ramada, or veranda, is the storage place of the ollas. The tribal winemaker is called and when he enters the roundhouse secret rites are undertaken which are known only to the community's patriarch. Depending upon the richness of the syrup and the desert temperature, it takes a week or more to make the ritual wine from the saguaro fruit. When the wine is finally ready, a rider is sent out through the community to inform all the families of the time set aside for the Rain-Making Ceremony.

On the appointed day the people gather at the roundhouse. The singing and dancing begin and continue all night, while within the roundhouse secret rites are performed over the wine. Then, soon after sunrise, four large sheets of canvas are spread in a wide circle in front of the ramada. On each canvas a group of elders from various Papago villages are seated, surrounded by men and boys. Three principal elders come into the ramada and each speaks quietly to the crowd. Then the wine boys come out into the burning sunlight bearing eight baskets filled with wine. These are offered first to the elders sitting on the canvas and then to the spectators. Songs asking for the blessing of rain are offered as the people drink the sacred wine and form a large circle.

Then, as it always does in July after the ceremony, it rains heavily.

DANCING INTO THE TWENTIETH CENTURY

MANY OF THE DANCES once performed by Indians no longer exist. Some of them have been lost because of Christian missionary repression, while others have simply fallen into disuse because they no longer reflect Indian life in the twentieth century. Other dances persist—but only as social forms because their significance has been clouded or lost, much as the European ritual called hopscotch survives today as a child's game, though as Curt Sachs points out in *World History of the Dance*, it was once a ritual act of considerable importance.

In their effort to move closer to the centers of power in nature, Indians often imitate and transform themselves into things of the natural world that invest them with strength and vision. They receive power through their songs. Through their dances they touch unknown and unseen elements which they sense in the world around them. It is perhaps an error to speak of the Indian *imitation* of animals because such actions are not designed for emulation but for transformation. Dancers of contemporary dance have rediscovered this same process: they do not simply *perform* the movements of a choreographer—they *become* the movements through an intense kinesthetic projection of feeling and ideas as pure body expression. It is a process difficult to describe, but for primal peoples such as Indians it is easy. "To us," an Indian explained, "the apple is a very complicated and mysterious thing. But for the apple tree it is easy."

Almost every aspect of Indian life has its counterpart in dancing and singing and is associated with ritual. There are dances for war, for peace, for victory, for joy, and for sorrow. There are dances for courtship and dances for fertility. Some rites are devoted to bringing rain, especially among agricultural people. Other dances, like the animal dances of hunting people, encourage success in the hunt, good fishing, or anything else that is crucial for Indian survival. The paraphernalia of ceremonies is extremely complex and requires great scrutiny in its preparation and maintenance, but the actual dances connected with rituals are rather simple. There are traditional set patterns for the dances, but the actual steps are far less elaborate than most non-Indians realize. True, many of the sacred dances are retained by special societies within the tribe which require careful rehearsal of ritual acts. It is also true that some of the steps are strenuous. But the elements of the dances that make them sacred and powerful are of a totally different order from the pyrotechnics of ballet, flamenco, or Hindu dance. The dance patterns reverberate with tradition reaching beyond Indian memory. The steps of Indian dances are executed with an inner grace and simplicity. It is the deep *involvement* of the dancer in the dance that is the source of magic, not the complexity of the motions. Most Indian dances are relaxed and balanced between consciousness and trance—perfectly controlled, dignified, and strangely remote even when the steps are extremely vigorous.

There are some unique characteristics in Indian dance: the steps tend to favor bent knees, with the body in an erect, straight posture. While the torso does not often move with the undulation seen in African dances, Indian dancers often make elaborate movements with their head, especially in animal dances. There is seldom any complex use of the arms except when the dancer is performing a subtle mimetic gesture or representing the soaring of eagles or the flight of the thunderbird.

There are dance steps that are especially predominant in social and ritual dances, although these are only a few of countless movements. These basic patterns are called the toe-heel step, the drag step, the stomp step, and the canoe step.

The *toe-heel step* is the most frequently seen and also the simplest of Indian dance steps. It is performed to a two-beat, with the accent on the first beat, *one*-two. On the accented beat the dancer touches the ground with the left toe, bringing the left heel down on the second, unaccented beat.

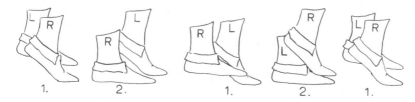

The *drag step* is another well-known Indian dance step, also based on a two-beat, but with the accent on the second beat: one-*two*. The dancer steps forward on the soft first beat, touching his toe to the ground. Then the foot is dragged backward and the heel is snapped down hard on the loud, second beat.

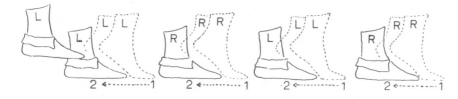

The *stomp step* is an energetic dance movement that is often found among the Pueblo dances of the Southwest. Normally it is performed with an upright body, the hands held closely to the body at the height of the hip. The drumbeat is a three-beat, with the accent on the first beat: *one*-two-three. On the first, loud beat the dancer lifts his knee high and brings his foot down hard with a stomping force. Then on the soft beats (two-three) he comes down on his toes in two quick hopping movements that make the rattles tied just below his knees reverberate with a marvelous sound.

The *canoe step* is a four-beat movement, with the accent on the first beat: *one*-two-three-four. On the first, accented beat the dancer steps on his left foot and then taps the right foot softly on the two-three-four beats. He then steps forward heavily with the right foot on the accented first beat.

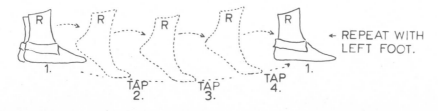

In its religious context Indian dance can be thought of as similar to the various ceremonial acts used by rabbis, priests, and ministers in marriage and burial rites. There are also many North American dances that have no religious significance, although they are definitely ceremonial in their tradition and performance. These dances and games are both playful and significant. The Handgame of the Kiowa, Kiowa Apache, and Comanche is typical of a social function which probably, at some remote time, had a strong and pointed religious basis. Today such dances and games are carried on as an embodiment of tribal unity and as an active sense of tradition. They retain a strong ceremonial function much as marriage ceremonies do for nonreligious white people. The Handgame of the Southern Plains is a "hide-and-seek," but it has all the outward functions of ceremony. It is a rite also known among the peoples of the Great Basin, Plateau, and Northwest Coast. There are many variations, but basically the game has two sides, one group hiding and the other guessing. It is called Handgame because a small marked bone or stick is concealed in the hand of the hider. Anyone who has ever considered Indians dour and lacking in humor should listen to recordings of Handgame songs or visit an event; they are filled with joy, laughter, and enormous enthusiasm.

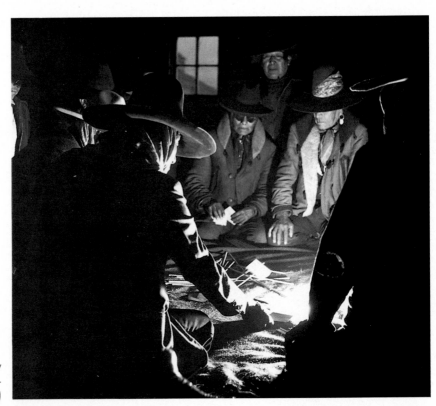

Shoshone Indians spend a wintry Sunday afternoon playing the stick game, a gambling game of the old days. (1968)

There are many other social dances, among them the very popular Fancy Dance of the Plains which most people have mistakenly grown to identify with *all* Indians and which is the prevalent dance at Indian intertribal meetings called powwows. Indians love to get together to exchange gossip and stories and to court one another…and it has been so from earliest times. The powwow is a Plains celebration which has spread to most of the other tribes. It is a good place to see Indian social dancing. There is often a rodeo, and a fair with cooking competitions, and a big dance

Indian rodeo in Bismarck, North Dakota.

The contemporary powwow retains traditional ceremonies and dances that are the core of North American Indian sensibility. Here, a singer and several drummers perform at a powwow in Fort Reno, Oklahoma.

Drummers from Tesuque Pueblo near Santa Fe perform the Buffalo Dance, a hunting rite, in headdresses adapted from the Plains tribes.

At a modern powwow, Indians in elaborate regalia perform the showy Fancy Dance. The costume and dance evolved from the old Grass Dance or Omaha Dance.

contest that climaxes the event. Many dances are performed by many tribes. The Fancy Dance is typical of the modifications of Indian culture produced by white influence. Based on the old Grass Dance or Omaha Dance (mistakenly called a War Dance by white and Indians alike), the Fancy Dance is very fast and active, involving elaborate steps and garish costumes that look as if the Follies had influenced the beautiful, subtle garb of the old Plains Indian. But there is no denying that the Fancy Dance—aniline-dyed chartreuse ostrich feathers, Hong Kong beadwork, and all—is a very impressive bit of contemporary entertainment among Indians. It is performed only by men.

Sport, like dance, has a supernatural impact for primal people. The major athletic contest of the Papago Indians is the kicking-ball race in which the contestant kicks a wooden ball before him as he runs. Such races were widespread in the Southwest and were connected with songs that were sung to assure victory. (1925)

Indian dance and ritual in the twentieth century have retained much of their original unifying influence upon tribal life. Today, as in the past, there have been dances that are largely social in function. Tournaments, races, and team games continue to interrelate the sacred and the secular. And the tenacious and famous holy rites of Southwestern Indians have their counterpart in the solemn Sun Dance of the Plains tribes. Behind all of these variations upon ancient ritual themes is the phenomenon of dance. Whether the various dances are apparently social or highly secretive and sacred, they have at their foundation the universal expressive power of movement which Indians recognize as the most significant manner in which the real world is revealed to them.

The Papago Indian Tcirkwena Dance held at San Xavier, Arizona. The ceremony, a blessing for rain and fertility, is performed by boys and girls trained to dance special steps while they carry effigies of birds, clouds, and rainbows. A series of eight songs, performed by a chorus of old men who are accompanied by basket drums and rasping sticks, make up the Tcirkwena cycle. The dance is often called the Skipping Dance, Season Dance, or Winter Rain Dance and is still offered by one village for the blessing of another, after which the performing guests are feasted and paid with gifts. (1925)

A Ponca Squaw Dance. The American flag can be seen faintly above dancers' heads. (1936)

Other dances involve both men and women. And women have also created their own modernization—a strange complication of the subtle stepping-in-place which used to represent the women's essential part in many dances. Today women do a type of Squaw Dance by themselves, consisting of large, dazzling steps, which look very much like the old Charleston, but which are performed to traditional drumming. Since it is really not a Squaw Dance it is sometimes called the Milk Shake Dance.

A fancy dancer in full regalia at an Oklahoma
powwow competition.
(1969)

Usually a Christmas celebration, the Matachines Dance of the Santa Clara Pueblo is a ceremony of mixed influences. There is no adequate explanation for the origin of the ceremony, though some Indians claim that it came from Montezuma in Mexico, while others believe it was brought from southern Europe. The music, very European in character, is performed by a Mexican fiddler. The costume, though different at each pueblo, incorporates Indian and European characteristics: a fringed Spanish shawl worn over a skirt, a scarf drawn over the face, a headdress resembling a bishop's miter. A decorated wooden trident is held in the left hand, and a rattle, concealed in a brightly colored scarf, in the right. One of the dancers, called Mananca, acts as leader. Malinche, a little girl dressed in a frock and a long white veil, also takes part, along with two mimes: a boy wearing the hide and head of a bull, and a man armed with a whip and a wooden knife.

The ceremony begins with a dance performed by the mitered men, the Matachines. Led by Mananca, they stand single file in two lines and face forward. Meanwhile, the Bull comes to life and a fearsome battle and slaughter follows between the old man with the whip and the Bull. During the combat, Malinche moves up and down between the lines of the imperturbable Matachines. The onlookers greet these mimes with shouts and laughter—indicating the humor of the combat. At the close of the ceremony, after the killing of the Bull, the Matachines kneel.

In Western society the act of payment is treated with discretion. But the procedures for giving monetary rewards and the customs of gift giving are not only highly visible among Indians but also have a very different significance from their context within the white world. Most ceremonies and even social gatherings provide an opportunity for complex honor dances and the highly public exchange of money and gifts. There is hardly a ritual that does not include or conclude in feasting and gift giving. Holy people who conduct ceremonies must be publicly compensated with gifts of blankets, money, or other valuables. And among some tribes, such as those of the Northwest Coast, the exchange of gifts is not simply a tangent of ceremonial life but a central thrust and focus of a complex social structure of rank and leadership.

The unifying character of the North West Coast was an obsession with property. The status symbol of wealth gave rise to the Potlatch—from the Nootka word *patshatl,* meaning "giving." Here a Kwakiutl chief proclaims his high station in an honor speech he delivers standing near a large pile of precious blankets. He will shortly give away the blankets to his audience, which is carefully seated according to rank. (1895)

Potlatches were grand social events to restore prestige, compete with peers, or celebrate honors. The central purpose was to demonstrate ultimate ostentation. One important man would give a Potlatch for a rival at which he gave away or destroyed publicly more riches than he hoped the rival could afford. One of the chief items of prestige was the blanket—and these were given away or burned by the hundreds. Then the rival would attempt to amass enough wealth to outdo the original Potlatch. Goods were even borrowed from outsiders, to be returned at a fixed rate of interest. Ultimately the Potlatch ceremony depleted the tribes, provoked quarrels, and was the major basis for the decline of the North West Coast people. Here, at a Potlatch at Quamichan, there is a blanket "scramble" as the "gifts" are tossed in the air.

The Sun Dance of the Plains

THE SUN DANCE is the most famous and spectacular of Plains Indian ceremonies. Yet it is rather young as a widespread tribal ritual and does not go back much before 1800. The devotion to a ritual which requires a large assembly of people was impossible on the Great Plains where the nomadic hunting culture forced the people to keep on the move in small bands which the meager food supplies could support. The summer hunt for buffalo which provided abundant meat for a large gathering depended upon the mobility of the horse-mounted hunter. Though the wild horse had once existed in America, it vanished long before the first Indians appeared in the Western hemisphere. The Spaniards introduced horses to America and fundamentally changed the cultural life of the Plains prior to 1600. The proud horsemen of the Indian nations of the Plains were originally rather humble planters, like the Cheyenne; or they were desert food gatherers, like the Comanche who invaded the Plains in search of buffalo only once they were mounted on stolen horses. It was two hundred years before northern bands such as the Dakota (Sioux) and Blackfeet had the use of the horse. But by 1800 the Plains area was reigned over by elegantly mounted hunters and warriors. The coming of the horse as well as the migration of tribes from desert areas and from the Great Lakes into the sparsely inhabited Plains gave way to itinerant settlements of nomadic hunters who used their abundance of meat and the leisure it provided to evolve soldier societies and medicine societies with ceremonial rites.

The Sun Dance celebrated this drastic change in the life-style of Plains Indians. It was essentially a new ceremony, though it was clearly built on the lines of many ancient rites. The name Sun Dance is Dakota. The Cheyenne call it the New Life Lodge, and the Ponca refer to it as the Sacred or Mystery Dance. With all these tribes the function of the Sun Dance was the renewal of communion with the earth, sun, and the supernaturals—especially the winds—in order that the tribe might have fertility, health, and continuing abundance of buffalo herds.

All Plains tribes practiced the Sun Dance, with the single exception of the Mandan—the people who probably inhabited the vast area of tall grass prior to the migration of many of the other tribes: Arapaho, Arikara, Assiniboin, Cheyenne, Crow, Hidatsa, Dakota, Ojibway, Arsi, Omaha, Ponca, Ute, Shoshone, Kiowa, and Blackfeet. Every group had variations in the way the ceremony was conducted, but a general form was consistent even among the tribes that still practice the rite.

The Sun Dance was usually performed during the late spring or early weeks of the summer. Usually the ceremony was annual, although that often depended on the vow of a tribesman to "build the lodge." The reasons for giving this vow were numerous. Among most of the tribes that depended upon a vow to initiate a Sun Dance, the most prevalent motive was a warrior's wish to take revenge for the death of a relative killed by an enemy. The idea that the Sun Dance was essentially a warrior's celebration of himself through heroic recounting of his deeds is very misleading. For many of the Plains people the Sun Dance was the supreme sacrament of religious life. Among the Blackfeet, for instance, the Sun Dance was initiated by a woman who sought the recovery of someone near death with illness. The assembly at the Sun Dance devoted itself to rituals to ensure the recovery of that sick person but also permitted the fulfillment of vows made to the sun by individual warriors at a time when they needed the power of the sun to rescue them from great peril.

The use of self-mutilation and torture has been exaggerated and used as the basis for banning the ceremony. For decades it was taken

[9]Major sources: George A. Dorsey, *The Cheyenne: The Sun Dance*, 1905; Frances Densmore, *Teton Sioux Music*, 1918.

for granted that the self-torture of the ceremony was a form of brutal self-sacrifice, but that notion now seems like a highly Christianized evaluation of the ritual as religious flagellation. It is more likely, as the Crows teach, that the sacrificing of one's body was aimed at softening the heart of divinities and bringing sympathetic help to humanity. Or as I understand it, and as it is taught by the Blackfeet, the severe trials of the ceremony are not intended to prove a man's bravery and his ability to withstand pain but rather to prove his great spirituality through his ability to be *unconscious* of and to transcend pain. This difference is crucial. It must be remembered that among Christians and Jews there is an effort not to *display* extreme emotions, while Indians attempt not to *feel*, let alone display, intense emotions. One viewpoint is a matter of appearances while the other is a matter of self-contained reality.

The Sun Dance is always held during the full moon. The people assemble at the encampment where it has been designated that the Sun Lodge will be built. All the clans and bands of the tribe come across the prairie day after day, converging on the encampment. There a great circle of tepees is made, usually arranged in a meticulous pattern determined by the hierarchy of the tribe. In the center of the circle is the ground where the Sun Lodge will be built. Around it are the tepees with their hundreds of cooking fires and handsome ponies. The people are dressed in their most elaborate and eloquent regalia, astride their finest horses, and gathered here and there for feasts with friends. Everywhere there are songs and laughter and the sounds of many drums. Social dances like the Grass Dance (or Omaha Dance), and games

like the Handgame amuse the vast assembly of people, who have not seen each other for an entire year. The Grass Dance is probably one of the oldest extant dances of the Plains. The same dance is called the War Dance or Fancy Dance in the Southern Plains, although it has never been performed in connection with war. It originated in Nebraska, probably among the Pawnee, although it is often attributed to the Omaha. The dance was originally called the Irushka by the Pawnee, named after the special headdress worn by the dancers, known in English as a hair roach and made from the tail of a deer. The Omaha made their own adaptation of the dance, inventing a bustle made of tied bunches of braided sweetgrass that they tucked under their belts to represent scalps—which were great victory prizes. The Omaha taught the dance to the Dakota, who in turn called it Peji Mgnaka Wacipi ("They Dance with Grass Tucked in Their Belts"). The grass bustles have been replaced with elaborate feathered bustles and complex beadwork belts.

Between the dances and games the Indians celebrate friendships by giving away tobacco, blankets, and even horses, both to friends and to the needy. These giveaways are a prominent part of the intertribal powwows of today.

Through all this merriment there is also a deep seriousness at the Sun Dance gatherings. Within many people the search for special favors is strong: for healing, for the settlement of old quarrels, for the hopes of good marriages, for victories, for fortune in the hunt and in life. These rites were outlawed by the government until 1935. Today the Sun Dance is performed once again, bringing great comfort and affirmation to its people.

FIRST DAY

ONE MAN stands out among the men who have assembled for the holiest of holy events, the Sun Dance. He is a renowned holy man called the lodge-maker who is acquainted with every detail of the ritual. It is he who conducts the entire ceremony, and it is this lodge-maker to whom everyone looks for instruction in a special tepee called the Preparatory Place. There is nothing to distinguish this tepee from all the others in the great circle, either in its structure, position, or the iconography painted on its lining. At dawn on the first day the name of the Preparatory Place is changed and designated as the Warriors' Tepee. The lodge-maker sings:

LODGEMAKER

On the warpath I give place to none;
With great unyielding courage I live my life.

All the men who have been lodge-makers in previous years assemble in the Warriors' Tepee, along with the new lodge-maker and his wife. When all have properly gathered, the tepee's name is again changed; it is now known as the Priests' Tepee.

SECOND DAY

VERY EARLY IN the morning the priests arise and feast themselves. Then the lodge-maker requests the assistance of all former holy men, and together they appoint the crier. When this selection of the man who will make the announcements to all those assembled at the Sun Dance has been made, the tepee is uprooted and carried a distance of fifty steps into the circle from the innermost point of the encampment. It now becomes known as the Lone Tepee. The lodge-maker's wife fetches her hoe and ritualistically clears the grass from the floor of the Lone Tepee, making what is called the Barren Earth. Now the priests assemble once again within the Lone Tepee, sitting on fresh sage, which the lodge-maker's wife has scattered about and covered with blankets. A pipe the lodge-maker has brought with him is placed on the cleared space in front of him and the assistant chief priest. Then the lodge-maker kneels at the side of the chief priest, who grasps the right hand of the lodge-maker so that his thumb is directed toward the ground just beyond the pipe. He then lowers the lodge-maker's thumb to the ground and rubs the earth in a circular motion, making a smooth place in the dirt which is called First Earth because it signifies the beginning of vegetable life.

Now the pipe is filled and lighted from live coals that have been brought into the tepee. After the pipe is lighted, the mouthpiece is directed toward the First Earth. Then the pipe is passed around the circle of priests, each directing its stem toward the First Earth before beginning to smoke.

Now the sacred bundle is placed on the ground before the lodge-maker. The assistant chief priest delicately takes it into his hands and carefully opens it, removing from it a buffalo-chip, a piece of sinew, and some braided sweet grass. Then the bundle is retied. The sinew is torn into five pieces, which are then balled up into pellets and pressed into the pipe—representing the buffalo which nourishes the people. Then additional pellets made from dried sweet grass are placed in the pipe, representing the vegetation that nourishes the buffalo. Two pinches of tobacco are taken from the tobacco bag and are pressed into the pipe. Then the pipe stem and bowl are painted red with four distinctive gestures. It is now time to form the Second Earth.

The crier arises and lifts a buffalo robe, which he gathers around himself. He is then painted, after which he puts on his moccasins and goes out among the people of the encampment, crying out to everyone.

CRIER

Sand-hill-men! Young Sand-hill men! Sutayo
*   Band! Big-Lodge-Men!*
Notiswahiswisti!
The lodge-maker has taken pity on you!
He gives you word that he relinquishes his
*   wife from the sacred lodge.*
He wishes to announce to all this great act he
*   has done for you!*

Men chosen for their importance in the tribe go into seclusion and dress in their finest regalia. They then assemble in order to go together in search of a suitable tree with a fork at the top which will serve as the center post of the great lodge. After finding the sacred tree, the warriors sing as they ceremonially paint the trunk.

WARRIORS

Father, all these he has made me own—
The trees and the forest standing in their
*   places.*

Now the site of the Sun Dance Lodge is selected by the priest appointed by the lodge-maker. The priest walks to the center of the encampment, and after carefully examining the earth, he selects a place where the lodge will be built. At the center of this sacred place he assembles a few sticks and places a bit of grass on top of them. This marks the place where the painted center pole will be erected once it has been cut and brought to the encampment.

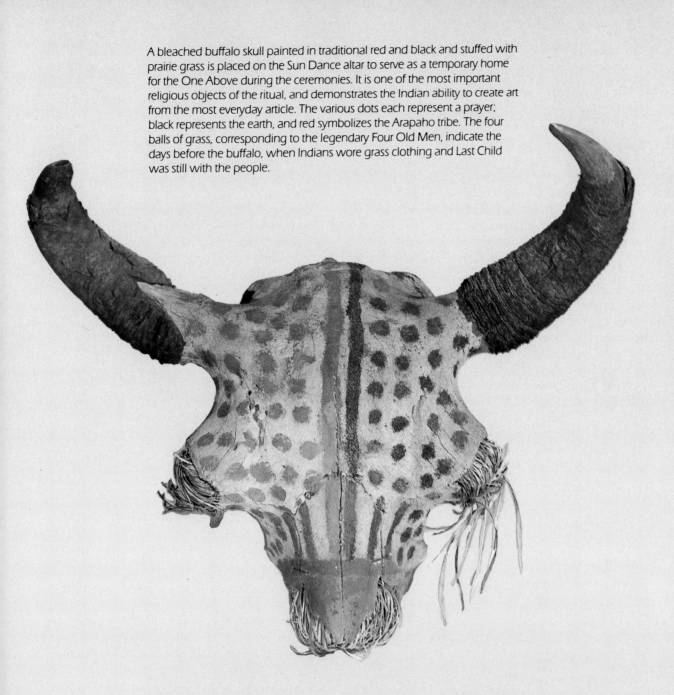

A bleached buffalo skull painted in traditional red and black and stuffed with prairie grass is placed on the Sun Dance altar to serve as a temporary home for the One Above during the ceremonies. It is one of the most important religious objects of the ritual, and demonstrates the Indian ability to create art from the most everyday article. The various dots each represent a prayer; black represents the earth, and red symbolizes the Arapaho tribe. The four balls of grass, corresponding to the legendary Four Old Men, indicate the days before the buffalo, when Indians wore grass clothing and Last Child was still with the people.

THIRD DAY

T HE PRIESTS ceremonially travel over the earth outside the Lone Tepee, smoking as they search the ground and consult each other. Then they make the Third Earth in a special place that has been very carefully selected. Returning to the Lone Tepee, they make the Fourth Earth, after which they are feasted. While the priests feast, one of the warriors who scouted for and painted the center pole approaches the tree a second time. He is clad in rich buckskin and wears his war-medicine paint. He rides alone to the sacred tree. Pausing just in front of it, he addresses it as he would a person, telling a heroic war story in which he recounts his greatest exploits against the enemy. Then, suddenly, he strikes the tree, just as if he had encountered and touched an enemy, which is the way that Indians "count coup."

Meanwhile an old buffalo skull is placed upside down in front of the Lone Tepee. The assistant chief priest goes up to the skull, approaching it four times before touching it. He ceremonially cleanses it of old age. He prays and then makes four passes toward the skull before he grasps it at the base of the horns, lifting it, and turning it toward the south, before lowering it to the ground. He steps over the skull, now lifts it again and carries it slowly toward the Lone Tepee. He deposits the skull inside the Lone Tepee and with the other priests makes the Fifth Earth.

FOURTH DAY

THE SECRET RITES in the Lone Tepee are performed by the lodge-maker and his wife. They prepare and paint the materials to be used in the construction of the Sun Dance altar, such as the buffalo skull, the center-pole image, the drumstick rattles, the earth peg, and the fire spoon. The sacred pipe is filled and made ready. By midday the priests have abandoned the Lone Tepee. Outside, the preparations for building the Sun Dance arbor are under way. Warrior societies have assembled the timbers, including the painted center pole, which has been ceremonially cut down. The priests join the warrior societies in erecting the Sun Dance lodge. Before raising the center pole, the priests put into the forked top a bundle of brush, a buffalo hide in the form of a human effigy, a buffalo hide effigy in the shape of a buffalo, and several long sticks with tobacco bags attached to them, as well as several other religious offerings. This completed collection of medicines in the form of a bundle is called the Eagle's or the Thunderbird's Nest. Now the center pole is raised.

WARRIORS AND PRIESTS

Sacred-I-stand-behold-me-was-said-to-me!

These words are the voice of the people. Again the pole speaks:

WARRIORS AND PRIESTS

At-the-center-of-earth-stand-looking-around-you;

Recognizing-the-people-stand-looking-around-you!

When the pole is raised the men sing:

MEN

Grandfather, at the places of the four winds may you be revered.

You made me wear something sacred.

—The tribe stands here in reverence because we wish to live.

Around the center pole is built a circular framework made of widely spaced posts. This structure is then covered with green branches. Within the enclosure a clearing is set aside as the altar, and traditionally painted buffalo skulls are placed upon it. The iconography imprinted on the skull is made in black, with various colors used to fill in the outlined images: yellow for the eagle's feet, purple for the spots

on the turtle. A crimson sun is then painted on a skull with yellow lines radiating from the center. Then a quarter moon is made, half in yellow and half in blue. Dark-red lines are made where each horn meets the buffalo skull. Tufts of sacred sage are then placed into the eye sockets and into the mouth of the skull. Now the priests enter the lodge and it is ceremonially dedicated. The crier calls to the societies, and the sun dancers begin to assemble in the lodge.

Before the main celebrants perform their Sun Dance, the eminent warriors of the tribe give dramatic presentations of their greatest military exploits. Then the young braves and warriors who have vowed to perform the Sun Dance enter the Lodge very slowly. They are purified by having fasted and gone without water or sex in preparation for being painted by their sponsors, who are called their grandfathers.

YOUNG WARRIORS

A voice I will send with my dance. Hear me!

The land, hear me!

A voice I am sending from all over.

Hear me and I will live!

PRIESTS

Grandfather, a voice I am going to send to you. Hear me!

All over the cosmos a voice I am going to send. Hear me!

Grandfather, I will live! I have said it!

Now the dance begins, with the celebrants blowing their whistles made from the wing bone of the eagle. They gaze at the center pole and move relentlessly in a simple step until all the demands of the Sun Dance vow have been fulfilled and the new sun arises on the final, sixth morning of the ceremony.

During the Sun Dance, three leaders of the Piegan band of the Blackfoot Indians—Spotted Eagle, Chief Elk, and Bull Child—blow eagle-bone whistles to assure good weather during the ceremony.

A young brave, connected to the center pole of the Sun Dance arbor by thongs attached to skewers in his breast, attempts to pull himself free by breaking the skewers through his flesh. Not all Plains tribes employ self-induced pain in the ceremony: the Utes, Shoshone, Arapaho, and Kiowa appear originally to have fasted and danced without any use of what ethnologists have called self-torture. The true point of the physical activities of the Sun Dance is actually closely related to the Western view of prayer rather than immolation or self-sacrifice.

FIFTH DAY

F OR EACH DANCE around the center pole the celebrants are freshly painted with specific patterns and colors.

DANCERS

Wakan tanka, when I pray to him black face paint he grants me.

During the fifth day some of the sun dancers are attached, at the breast or back, with skewers which pierce their muscles. These skewers are attached by rawhide thongs to the top of the center pole.

The Sun Dance step is quite basic: the dancers lift their toes rhythmically one after the other while blowing bone whistles and pulling against the thongs tied to the center pole. The dancers move slowly in a circle around the pole as they pull and tug against the pole until they tear themselves loose, or exhausted, are released by the dance leader.

SIXTH DAY

S EVERAL DIFFERENT painted patterns are drawn one after another on the sun dancers' bodies on the final day. The costume is traditional: wreaths of sage are worn on the head, rings of sage are held in the hand, and sage is also tied to the wrists. The dancers wear skirts of painted hide or beaded blan-

kets reaching from their waists to their ankles. Some tribes also wear chains of beads over their shoulders and plumes in their hair, while others use rabbit skins and quilled falls tied to the back of their heads.

The eagle-bone whistles make a curious sound that is the source of all power. A white plume of the eagle is attached to the end of the whistle so it is blown forward by the dancer's breath-of-life. Each whistle is painted with red, green, blue, and yellow lines and dots representing the keen sense of the eagle.

At the close of the Sun Dance the priests set aside time for those who wish to give gifts to the poor and to reward someone for a special kindness. Another final activity is the renaming of men who have earned new titles in battle or through some other achievements. Then on the final morning, before the sun rises, the dancers sing:

DANCERS

May the sun rise well; may the earth appear bright!
May the moon rise well; may the earth appear bright!
Father, all these he has made me own.
The trees and the forest standing in their place.

As the sun appears over the horizon the dance is ended with a song.

PRIESTS

Here am I, look at me: I am the Sun!
Look upon me!
Here I am, look at me!
I am the Moon, look upon me!

When the Sun Dance is ended, the sacred paraphernalia is carefully collected, wrapped, and taken away by the keepers of the bundles. Only the lodge is left, where the wind and the snow can sweep through its rustling branches. Long afterward, whenever the dancers pass the sacred lodge, they recall the vows they made and the feasting and blessings that were give to them.

DANCERS

Where, holy you behold,
In the place where the Sun rises,
Holy, may you behold this holiness.
Where, holy, you see
In the place where the Sun passes us
in its course,
Holy, may you see it.
Where goodness you see,
At the turning back of the Sun,
Goodness, may you see it and live!

THE GHOST DANCE

O NE DAY IN 1890, during an eclipse of the sun, Wovoka had a vision. The son of an Indian prophet, he had been brought up by a white family and given the name Jack Wilson. News of his vision quickly filtered among the hopeless, dispossessed tribes and sparked a great revival of passion and independence.

Wovoka proclaimed his revelations: a spirit would come and raise all the dead, the buffalo would once again roam in abundance on the plain, and the white intruders would be driven from the continent by a great flood. This spirit, the force of the cosmos, that loves the Indian people, had vowed to save them. This spirit had given Wovoka a dance called the Ghost Dance to teach to the people, and through its ritual many thousands of Indians hoped to be saved from their terrible defeat.

Of all the tribes fascinated by this prophecy, the mystical Dakota embraced it

Pawnee Ghost Dance shirt. Sacred icons are
painted on the buckskin. (ca. 1890)

most ardently. They grew to believe that the costume of the ceremony, the Ghost Shirt, would protect them from the white man's bullets.

Indians gathered in great numbers, and everywhere they gathered, they danced with the passion of a dying people. Their bodies, minds, and feelings merged in such an ecstasy of revelation that white people became frightened; they saw in this new ritual the possibility of a revival of hostilities. It was the ritual they feared, for the ritual could be held anywhere. It could light up Indian hopes, give comfort and solidarity, and provide courage. Indian guns and arrows were no longer the threat. The danger for whites was the power of ceremonial dance, a magic they could not control.

Almost by error the Dakota leader, Sitting Bull, was killed while a prisoner of war. As a result, his distraught people were further impassioned by the promises of the Ghost Dance. A band of three hundred Indians led by Big Foot were on their way to the Badlands, where their tribe was dancing, when they were captured by the cavalry and marched toward the government agency. On the first night they camped in a hollow near a creek called Wounded Knee.

In the morning when the people awakened, they discovered Hotchkiss guns stationed on the hill and cavalrymen lining the banks surrounding the encampment. But the Indians were not afraid. They knew their Ghost Shirts would protect them. Ordered to relinquish their weapons, the Indians refused. The soliders went among them, searched them, and disarmed them.

Then a single shot was fired.

The Hotchkiss guns opened up, firing rapidly at close range, directly into the assembled, unarmed people. In a very few moments the snowy ground turned red. The Dakota fell like leaves in a terrible wind. Their bodies were torn and broken beneath the miraculous shirts that failed to protect them. Those who ran in terror were pursued and gunned down. Women, children, the old, and the young. And when the snow began to fall, the dead were frozen into a grotesque sculpture in the desolate, surreal landscape. They would not rise again.

The Seventh Cavalry was awarded twenty-six congressional medals of honor for their part on this action.

In that forlorn valley in South Dakota and everywhere across Indian lands, the songs of the Ghost Dance are imprinted like the rings of an ancient tree.

The wind stirs the willows.
The wind stirs the grasses.
Fog! Fog!
Lightning!
Whirlwind!
The rocks are ringing,
They are ringing in the mountains.
Now the sun's beams are running out,
The sun's yellow rays are running out.

We shall live again.

The encampment for a Cheyenne-Arapaho Ghost Dance—two
miles northwest of Fort Reno, Oklahoma. (1889)

3
THE BLESSING

# We Shall Live Again!

IT WILL NOT HAPPEN AGAIN. The struggle for a separate reality and a separate existence is visible everywhere in Indian America, an island world in a sea of alien influences. I have spent much of my life traveling through that special America. What has impressed me and depressed me most is the fact that most of what I have seen is slowly passing out of existence. This is not to say that Indians are giving up their identity (quite the contrary), but the stress of alienation from the majority, the influx of technology, and the outpouring of the majority's messages through the media have their effect. For instance, what I discovered among the Hopi people is a fragile transitional moment precariously balanced between old and new worlds. It will surely impress anyone who ventures into Hopiland to take part in that moment, for it allows you to get close to something that would normally stay out of reach, like a swift, free beast in the field. You may freely wander among the spectacular valleys and villages of native people like a traveler in some romantic dream, passing safely among primal people who stop to stare at you intently, curiously but unthreateningly. Their eyes are filled with something special, something with which Europeans have been out of touch since the time of Descartes. It will not happen again. You are unique in sharing the experience of these first Americans, just as they are in providing it. It cannot happen again. This is surely the last generation for which the world of the ancients remains alive and wholly visible.

The most tenacious aspect of Indian life is ritual and the long-remembered ideals which it both conceals and celebrates. In dress, housing, employment, and all the other external traits of civilization, the Indian is almost indistinct from other Americans. The rich residue of ancient Indian culture lives on in the ceremonial, the intangible ideas and tribal practices of dance.

If we accept the paradox that our essential humanity is understood through cultural differences rather than cultural similarities, then it is possible that the ceremonial life of Indians embodies an enduring and luminous insight into something so fundamentally human that many of us have lost track of it in our devastating intent upon uniformity and equality. At the core of everyone's culture is a package of beliefs which every child learns and which has been culturally determined long in advance of our birth. The world is rendered coherent by our description of it. What we see when we speak of reality is simply that description. At the core of white experience is a condition of culture which insists that what is described is absolute, whereas at the core of Indian viewpoint is the assumption that reality is not an absolute. Native Americans see and experience many separate realities. They believe in a multi-verse, or a bi-verse, but not the uni-verse of Western civilization.

Assiniboin Indian holding sacred eagle. Photo by Edward S. Curtis. (1926)

This singularity of the cosmos is a conviction of the dominant race with which it seems persistently uncomfortable. Ever since the ecstatic mystery rites of pre-Socratic Greece declined, Western civilization has been continually challenged by the dream of escaping its own framework: the categorical, the linear, and the eternally fixed and knowable. The forward plunge of civilization, which some look upon as progress, has brought the impulse to express feelings too rigidly under the domination of reason, and this, in turn, has caused whites to think of themselves predominantly as perpetual spectators of the world, afraid to create their own forms because they might fall outside the conventional description of reality. Until very recently white people were cut off from their own bodies and from expressive activities by their own constraint and embarrassment. They lacked a body that could function in harmony with their ideas and feelings. Consequently they were reassured of the Christian assessment of the body as a liability and as an organism over which they possessed little control. Without an articulate body, without facial movement which genuinely reflects states of mind, without a torso which responds to self and relates to external events, people cannot participate in their world or in their own emotional lives.

The perfectly coordinated, lavishly expressive body of the ceremonial dancer is unmistakably different from the prim, stiff, and fashionably prancing body of the ballroom dancer. In the ceremonial performer there is an idealized transparency, a configuration in which the totality of human experience is visible. The feelings intrinsic to ritual are probably no more fundamental or primitive than the loftiest sentience of any of the Western arts. For primal peoples dance (or, in reality, the larger social organism called ceremony) perfectly embodies the most commonplace and the most elevated ideas.

Martha Graham, who devoted so much of her life to ritualizing contemporary experience, said that dance is stupendously simple, which is what makes it so difficult for modern people to comprehend. The idea of the *spiritual body* is equally simple. If there were better words to describe such a phenomenon, perhaps it would be easier to say what I am saying, but in that case I seriously doubt that there would be any reason to talk about ritual, ceremony, and dance in the first place. There is nothing really "spiritual" in the concept of the spiritual body, but there isn't another word that suggests all the qualities of nobility, loftiness of thought, and intensity of ideals and feelings which we normally exclude from our connotation of "body." The concept behind the term spiritual body does not envision just the anatomical body but all the still-mysterious physiology by which the body experiences itself and the world, the amplification of the senses and the puzzling process of perception and thought by which brain recreates itself as mind.

When the worlds of whites and Indians collided, there was more involved than a militaristic confrontation of a primitive culture and a civilization. We can no longer talk of civilization so facilely, and we cannot uphold the ethnocentric notion that there are only two worlds: one that is civilized and creative and another that is savage and destructive. Unlike any prior confrontation (even that of East and West or the invasion of Africa by whites or the conflict of Islam and Christianity), the meeting of Indians and non-Indians represented two utterly alien forces with differences so fundamental that it is impossible to grasp fully the philosophical explosiveness of the situation.

A fool dancer rests and smokes a clay
pipe, his mask pushed back atop his head.

Indians were overwhelmed by the invaders. But subjugation is not necessarily the same as assimilation. Even though the ancient Romans conquered the Greeks and were the dominant group both in numbers and power, the Roman world became thoroughly Hellenic. It is possible in this way for a people to be overwhelmed physically but not culturally. And even where conquest results in the gradual alteration of most of what is apparently unique in the culture of the defeated people, it is possible that their vision of reality and destiny and of themselves and their world will remain surprisingly untouched. That is what has happened to the American Indian. As tribal lands were lost, as social systems were torn open and customs were suppressed, an initial wave of hopelessness and apathy settled over the people. Then gradually something began to happen: revivalist and messianic movements sprang up in countless places where beaten Indians were drawn to the words of holy men who promised the return of the old days and the affirmation of the quintessential realm of Indians.

But Native Americans are not alone in their hope for the rebirth of a strong, life-supporting mythology. There are many people of many races whose power resides in one of the few facilities of intelligence in which the West has had little aptitude or awareness. In the articulation of the spiritual body, in the overlay of ancient and ultramodern mentalities a new expertise and creative force has been emerging for more than one hundred years. Rituals which resound with great antiquity and power are being revived and newly created: ceremonies and myths that celebrate the past as well as the present. In their most nostalgic as well as their most avant-garde forms, these rites transcend ethnicity and become metaphors of the relentless tensions that exist between the ceremonial life of a people and the universality of human experience.

We do not have the sun within us, and yet we must have a light so we can find our way through the darkness. Our rituals illuminate and, finally, define our reality. Technology gives us mechanisms for meticulous observation, but the light by which we truly *see* is a mythic lantern. And the world that it lights is the realm of ritual by which we know ourselves and what we have been and what we are becoming. Native American ceremonial life is such a light. Through it we understand that nothing brings us closer to reality than our willingness to sacrifice "truth" for the wholly imaginal expression of the only rituals left to us—those that flow from whatever it is within us that we call "ourselves."

Hopi Indian maidens watching the dancers. (1906)

CALENDAR OF INDIAN EVENTS

Some Indian practices and concepts differ from those of non-Indians. It is therefore possible that certain manners which white people find acceptable may be offensive to Indians, and vice versa. If you are going to visit Indians, especially if you plan to view their ceremonies and dances, you must respect their beliefs. Remember that all Indians understand English, though they may not willingly speak it. It is a good idea to keep remarks to yourself. Native Americans are generally more "sensitive" people than other Americans, and they have very definite ideas about what is and what is not humorous about being Indian. It is important not to talk loudly, and it is also a good idea not to point with your hands—practices Indians usually find offensive.

Indian settlements (with very rare exceptions) are not tourist attractions; they are traditional homes of Indian people, and the land surrounding their often ancient domain is sacred to them. White people are allowed to visit these places because of the graciousness of the owners. If you are invited into a house, by all means enter, but do not go in if you are not invited. If food is offered, eat at least a bit of it, since refusal can be seen as an insult. If an Indian presents a gift, make certain that an exchange courtesy of some kind is made in due time—though it is wise not to offer money but rather something that has some personal value to you.

Try to be extremely cautious about asking questions: Indians have a very special idea of privacy. Personal questions and questions about rites, dances, and costumes should be avoided. It's better to do your own research before or after your visit and simply take in everything you can while witnessing events. It is extremely important that you *never* take any photographs or make any notes, sketches, recordings, or drawings without specific permission from the chairman or chief of the Indian settlement. Even if permission is granted, be certain to ask consent before taking anyone's photograph. A small fee is normally expected for the privilege of taking someone's photograph. If permission is not granted to take photographs during a dance, it is wise to put your camera away, out of sight. It is a good rule of conduct to behave among Indians and at their homes as you would in a church or synagogue: stay out of the way, do not applaud ceremonies or dances even if the Indians do, be as inconspicuous as possible, presume you are in a foreign nation, but remember that the Indians understand your comments and facial expressions.

The following is a list of Native American ceremonial events around the country by general geographic area, the approximate time of year, the place and name of the event.

SOUTHWEST

_____

New Year's Day	. . Most pueblos, N. Mex., Ariz.	*Corn, Turtle, and other dances*
Early	. . . . . Most pueblos, N. Mex., Ariz.	*King's Day Inauguration*
Late	. . . . . . San Ildefonso, N. Mex.	*Buffalo and Comanche dances and feast*
	Hopi villages, Ariz.	*Kiva and Buffalo dances*
Late, or early Feb.	Acoma Pueblo, N. Mex.	*Governor's Fiesta*

FEBRUARY _____

Early	. . . . . Cochiti, Santo Domingo, San Felipe pueblos, N. Mex.	*Buffalo dances and Candlemas Celebration*
	Taos Pueblo, N. Mex.	*Los Comanches*
Middle	. . . . San Juan Pueblo, N. Mex.	*Special dances*
Late	. . . . . . San Juan Pueblo, N. Mex.	*Clan dances*
	Isleta Pueblo, N. Mex.	*Evergreen dances*
	Hopi villages, Ariz.	*Bean dances in kivas*

MARCH _____

Early	. . . . . St. John's Mission, Gila River Reservation, Ariz.	*Indian Dance Festival*
Middle	. . . . Sacaton, Ariz.	*Mul-Chu-Tha Fair and Rodeo*
	Old Laguna Pueblo, N. Mex.	*St. Joseph's Feast Day*
Late	. . . . . . Cochiti Pueblo, N. Mex.	*Keresan dances*
	Ignacio and Towoac, Colo.	*Bear Dance, Spring Welcome*
	Salt River Reservation, Ariz.	*Pima Trade Fair and dances*
	Fort Yuma Reservation, Calif.	*Yuma (Quechan) Tribal Powwow*

APRIL _____

Easter	. . . . . Pascua, Tucson, Ariz.	*Yaqui dances and pageant*
	Most pueblos, N. Mex.	*Celebration of Opening of Irrigation Ditches*

	Most pueblos, N. Mex.	*Easter ceremonies, footraces*
	Yaqui Village, Tucson, Ariz.	*Festival of St. Francis*
After Easter . .	Most pueblos	*Spring ceremonies*
Early	All pueblos, N. Mex., Ariz.	*Spring Corn dances*
	Northern Ute, Fort Duchesne, Utah	*Bear Dance*
Late	University of New Mexico, Albuquerque, N. Mex.	*Intertribal dances*
	San Xavier Reservation, Tucson, Ariz.	*Powwow*

MAY ——

Early	San Felipe Pueblo, N. Mex.	*Feast Day and Corn Dance*
	Taos Pueblo, N. Mex.	*Corn Dance and ceremonial dances*
	Cochiti Pueblo, N. Mex.	*Corn Dance*
Middle	Taos Pueblo, N. Mex.	*San Ysidro Fiesta*
Late	Tesuque Pueblo, N. Mex.	*Spring dances*
	Southern Ute Reservation, Colo.	*Bear Dance*
	Pala Reservation, Calif.	*Corpus Christi Festival*
Memorial . . . Day	Morongo Reservation, Calif.	*Malki Spring Festival*
	Havasupai Reservation, Ariz.	*Indian dances*
	Flagstaff, Ariz.	*Indian Fair*

JUNE ——

Early	Sacaton, Ariz.	*Yaqui Pageant*
	Ute Mountain, Towaoc, Colo.	*Bear Dance*
	Santa Clara Pueblo, N. Mex.	*Buffalo Dance*
Middle	Sandia Pueblo, N. Mex.	*Feast and Corn Dance*
	Taos, Santa Clara, San Juan pueblos, N. Mex.	*San Antonio Day*

	Leavitt Reservation, Janesville, Calif.	*Bear Dance*
	San Carlos Reservation, Peridot, Ariz.	*Apache ceremonials*
Late	San Juan, Taos, Isleta, Cochiti, Laguna, and Acoma pueblos, N. Mex.; Papago Reservation, Ariz.	*San Juan's Day*
	Tule River Reservation, Calif.	*San Juan's Day*
	Jemez Pueblo, N. Mex.	*Rooster Pull*
	Acoma, Isleta, Laguna, Santa Ana, San Juan, and Taos pueblos, N. Mex.	*San Pedro's Day*

JULY _____

Early	Window Rock, Ariz.	*Indian rodeo*
	Mescalero Apache Reservation, N. Mex.	*Mountain Spirits Ceremony*
	Nambe Pueblo, N. Mex.	*Waterfall Ceremony*
	Most pueblos, N. Mex., Ariz.	*Feasts, games, races*
	Walker River Reservation, Shurz, Nev.	*Fiesta*
	Duck Valley Reservation, Owyhee, Nev.	*Feast and games*
Middle	Jaynesville, Calif.	*Bear Dance*
	Cochiti Pueblo, N. Mex.	*Feast, Green Corn Dance*
	Mission San Diego de Alcala, San Diego, Calif.	*Festival of Bells*
Late	Fallon, Nev.	*All-Indian Celebration*
	Taos Pueblo, N. Mex.	*Corn Dance*
	Santa Ana and Laguna pueblos, N. Mex.	*Santiago's Day Dances*
	Cochiti Pueblo, N. Mex.	*Corn Dance*

Acoma and Santo Domingo pueblos, N. Mex.	*Rooster Pull*
Santa Ana and Acoma pueblos, N. Mex.	*Feast Day and Corn Dance*
Santa Clara Pueblo, N. Mex.	*Puye Ceremonial*
Hopi villages, Ariz.	*Niman Kachina*
Southern Ute Reservation, Colo.	*Sun Dance*
Ute Mountain Reservation, Colo.	*Sun Dance*
Uintah and Ouray Reservation, Duchesne, Utah	*Sun Dance*
Papago Reservation, Ariz.	*Sajuaro Festival*

AUGUST ————————————————————————————————

Early	Jemez Pueblo, N. Mex.	*Old Pecos Bull Dance*
	Santo Domingo Pueblo, N. Mex.	*Fiesta, Ripe Corn Dance*
	Picuris Pueblo, N. Mex.	*Feast Day*
	Acoma and Laguna pueblos, N. Mex.	*San Lorenzo Day, Corn Dance*
Middle	Santa Clara Pueblo, N. Mex.	*Santa Clara Day*
	Mesita Village, Laguna Pueblo, N. Mex.	*Feast of St. Anthony, dances*
	Zia Pueblo, N. Mex.	*Assumption Day, Corn dances*
Late	Supai, Ariz.	*Havasupai Peach Festival*
	Santa Fe, N. Mex.	*Annual Indian Market*
	Isleta Pueblo, N. Mex.	*Spanish Fiesta*
	All Hopi pueblos, Ariz.	*Snake Dance*
	Peach Springs, Ariz.	*Hualapai Powwow*

Labor Day . . . Weekend	Whiteriver, Ariz.	*Apache Fair, Crown Dance*
Early	Acoma Pueblo, N. Mex.	*St. Stephen's Day, Corn Dance*
	Whiteriver, Ariz.	*Apache Fair*
	Isleta Pueblo, N. Mex.	*St. Augustine's Day, dances*
	Window Rock, Ariz.	*Navajo Tribal Fair*
	San Ildefonso Pueblo, N. Mex.	*Pinnhut Festival*
Middle	Southern Ute Reservation, Colo.	*Tribal Fair, dances*
	Jicarilla Apache Reservation, N. Mex.	*Ghost Dance, fiesta*
	Tuolumne, Calif.	*Acorn Festival*
	Laguna Pueblo, Old and New, N. Mex.	*Fiesta and social dances*
Late	Laguna Pueblo, Old and New, N. Mex.	*Fiesta and social dances*
	Taos Pueblo, N. Mex.	*Sundown Dance*
	Taos Pueblo, N. Mex.	*San Geronimo Feast Day*
	San Juan Pueblo	*Fiesta and Harvest Dance*
	Isleta Pueblo, N. Mex.	*Evergreen Dance*
	Tuba City, Ariz.	*Indian Fair*
	Shiprock, N. Mex.	*Navajo Fair*

Early	Papago Reservation, Ariz.	*Feast of St. Francis*
	Nambe Pueblo, N. Mex.	*Elk Dance, fiesta*
Middle	Laguna Pueblo, N. Mex.	*Harvest dances celebration*
Late	Most pueblos, N. Mex., Ariz.	*Ceremonial dances*

NOVEMBER _____

Early	. . . . .	Papago Reservation, Ariz.	*All-Indian Tribal Fair and Rodeo*
Middle	. . . .	Jemez Pueblo, N. Mex.	*Harvest Fiesta, Corn dances*
		Tesuque Pueblo, N. Mex.	*Feast Day, Buffalo dances*
		Peridot, Ariz.	*Apache Memorial for Veterans*
Late	. . . . . .	Parker, Ariz.	*Tribal Thanksgiving*

DECEMBER _____

Early	. . . . .	San Xavier, Ariz.	*St. Francis Feast*
		Zuni Pueblo, N. Mex.	*Shalako Kachina Ceremony*
Middle	. . . .	Las Cruces, N. Mex.	*Celebration, Tortugas Indians*
		Jemez Pueblo, N. Mex.	*Matachine Dance*
Late	. . . . . .	Colorado River Reservation, Parker, Ariz.	*Indian Water Festival*
		All Rio Grande pueblos	*Night bonfires, processions*
Christmas Week	. . .	All pueblos, N. Mex., Ariz.	*Midnight Mass, dancing in churches*
		Most pueblos, N. Mex., Ariz.	*Deer and Matachine dances*
		Colorado River reservations, Parker, Ariz.	*Christmas Tree for Tribes*
		San Juan Pueblo, N. Mex.	*Turtle Dance*
		Sandia Pueblo, N. Mex.	*Deer Dance*

CENTRAL PLAINS

MAY _____

Summer Saturdays	. . . .	Lower Brule, S. Dak.	*Calf roping*
Early	. . . . .	Tahlequah, Okla.	*Cherokee Village*
		Tahlequah, Okla.	*Cherokee Homecoming*

	Encampments at Wounded Knee, Kyle, Oglala, Allen, Porcupine, and Manderson, S. Dak.	*Powwows and dances*
Memorial Day Weekend	Black River Falls, Wis.	*Winnebago Powwow*
	Devil's Lake Reservation, Fort Totten, N. Dak.	*Powwow and dances*

JUNE _____

June	White Earth Reservation, Minn.	*Centennial Celebration and Occupancy*
June	Turtle Mountain Reservation, N. Dak.	*Sun Dance*
Evenings, . . . all summer	Chicago Indian Center, Chicago, Ill.	*Intertribal ceremonies*
	Red Lake Reservation, Minn.	*Powwow, Fish Fry*
Mid June– . . . late Aug.	Hot Springs, S. Dak.	*Crazy Horse Pageant*
	Tahlequah, Okla.	*"Trail of Tears"—Cherokee drama*
June–Labor . . Day, daily	Wisconsin Dells, Wis.	*Chippewa Powwow*
June–Labor . . Day, Tues. and Thurs.	Lac du Flambeau, Wis.	*Stand Rock Indian Powwow*
June–Labor . . Day, Sat.	Fort Thompson, S. Dak.	*Powwow*
Early	Belcourt, N. Dak.	*Sun Dance, Grass Dance*
Middle	White Cloud, Kan.	*Iowa Tribe Powwow*
	Fort Yates, N. Dak.	*Powwow*
	Pawhuska, Okla.	*Osage dances*
	Kyle, S. Dak.	*Powwow*
	Grass Mountain, S. Dak.	*Powwow*
	Clinton, Okla.	*Intertribal Powwow*

Late	Hominy, Okla.	*Osage ceremonial dances*
	El Reno, Okla.	*Intertribal Exposition*
	Rosebud, S. Dak.	*Spotted Tail Memorial Celebration*
	8 mi. W. of Horton, Kans.	*Kickapoo Powwow*
	Murrow Dance Grounds, Binger, Okla.	*Caddo Tribal Dance*

JULY ──

Every . . . . . . Saturday	Anadarko, Okla.	*Indian ceremonials*
Summer . . . . season	Hayward, Wis.	*Indian Dance*
	Indian Centers, Milwaukee, Wis.	*Oneida Indian Club Powwow*
Early	Sisseton, S. Dak.	*Sioux Ceremonial*
	La Creek, S. Dak.	*Powwow*
	Cannonball, N. Dak.	*All-Indian Powwow*
	Pawnee, Okla.	*Pawnee Powwow*
	Parmelee (Rosebud Reservation), S. Dak.	*Sun Dance*
	Spring Creek (Rosebud Reservation), S. Dak.	*Sioux Powwow*
	Carnegie, Okla.	*Kiowa Gourd-Clan Dance*
	Greenwood, S. Dak.	*Struck-by-the-Ree Powwow*
	Fort Thompson, S. Dak.	*Powwow dances*
	Hayward, Wis.	*Gathering of Tribes*
	Redlake, Minn.	*Indian Dancing Contest*
	Binger, Okla.	*Caddo Indian Dance*
	Cannonball, N. Dak.	*Powwow*
	Fort Cobb, Okla.	*Indian ceremonials*

Middle	Jim Thorpe Park, near Stroud, Okla.	*Sac and Fox Powwow*
	Mission, S. Dak.	*Antelope Powwow*
	Flandreau, S. Dak.	*Santee Sioux Powwow*
	Stomp Grounds, Gore, Okla.	*Red Bird Smith Birthday Celebration*
	New Town, N. Dak.	*Mandan Powwow*
Late	Ball Club, Minn.	*Chippewa Thanks for Wild Rice*
	Cherry Creek, S. Dak.	*Powwow*
	Mayetta, Kan.	*Potawatomi Powwow*
	Stomp Grounds, Red Rock, Okla.	*Oto-Missouri Powwow*
	Little Eagle, Standing Rock Reservation, S. Dak.	*Powwow*
	Belcourt, N. Dak.	*Powwow*
	N. of Red Rock (Noble County), Okla.	*Oto-Missouri Powwow*
	Ed Mack Farm, Shawnee, Okla.	*Sac and Fox Powwow*
	Pine Ridge, S. Dak.	*Oglala Sioux Sun Dance*

AUGUST —————————————————————————————

Early	Pine Ridge, S. Dak.	*Sun Dance*
	Tokio, N. Dak.	*Buffalo Dance*
	Fort Cobb, Okla.	*Indian ceremonials*
	Fort Yates, N. Dak.	*Powwow*
	Talihina, Okla.	*Choctaw Fair*
	Lower Brule, S. Dak.	*Indian Fair and Powwow*
Middle	Rosebud, S. Dak.	*Spotted Tail Powwow*
	Bull Head, S. Dak.	*Powwow*

	Macy, Nebr.	*Omaha Indian Homecoming*
	Parshall (Mountrail County) N. Dak.	*Reservation Fair*
	White Eagle, Okla.	*Ponca Indian Fair*
	Rosebud, S. Dak.	*Powwow*
Late	Rosebud, S. Dak.	*Tribal Fair, Powwow*
	Vineland, Minn.	*Mille Lacs Chippewa Powwow*
	Belcourt, N. Dak	*Annual Powwow*
	Canton, Okla.	*Arapaho Powwow*
	Fort Thompson, S. Dak.	*Powwow*
	Eagle Butte, S. Dak.	*Cheyenne River Fair*

SEPTEMBER ———————————————————————————

Labor Day . . . Weekend	Sisseton, S. Dak.	*Sioux Powwow*
	Nett Lake, Minn.	*Wild Rice Harvest*
	Devils Lake, Fort Totten, N. Dak.	*Sioux Fair and Powwow*
	Colony, Okla.	*Cheyenne-Arapaho Powwow*
	Fort Totten, N. Dak.	*Fair, Sioux Powwow*
	Colony, Okla.	*Tribal Powwows*
	Lawton, Okla.	*Gourd Dance Celebration*
	Black River Falls, Wis.	*Winnebago Powwow*
Sept.–May . .	YMCA, St. Paul, Minn.	*Indian Center Powwow*
Early	Bull Creek, S. Dak.	*Powwow*
	Soldier Creek, S. Dak.	*Powwow*
	Carnegie, Okla.	*Kiowa Powwow*
	Tama, Iowa	*Mesquakie Powwow*

	Anadarko, Okla.	*Mopope Powwow*
	Tahlequah, Okla.	*Cherokee National Holiday*
	Eagle Butte, S. Dak.	*Sioux Fair*
Middle	New Town, N. Dak.	*Tribal Arts and Crafts Fair*
Late	Oklahoma City, Okla.	*Annual American Indian Ceremonial Dance*
	Hominy, Okla.	*Tribal dances*
	Wamblee, S. Dak.	*Powwow*

OCTOBER _____

Weekends . . .	Danbury, Wis.	*Mille Lac Powwow*
	Eastlake, Wis.	*Chippewa dances*
	Vineland, Minn.	*Ceremonial dances*
Early	Fort Totten, N. Dak.	*Sioux Coronation*
	Pawnee, Okla.	*Pawnee Bill Art Show*

NOVEMBER _____

Middle	Carnegie, Okla.	*Kiowa Powwow*
	Indian City, Anadarko, Okla.	*Veterans Day Powwow*
	Pawhuska, Okla.	*Osage Indian Veterans Day*
	Greenwood, S. Dak.	*Struck-by-the-Ree Powwow*
	Carnegie, Okla.	*Kiowa Veterans Celebration*

NORTHWEST

JANUARY _____

New Year's Day . .	White Swan, Wash.	*Tribal New Year*
Varies	Tulalip Reservation, Wash.	*Treaty Day Feast*

FEBRUARY _____

Middle	Kamiah, Idaho	*Nez Percé war dances*
	Pendleton, Oreg.	*Umatilla Lincoln's Day*

Late	Toppenish, Wash.	*George Washington Celebration*
	Lapwai, Idaho	*Nez Percé Washington Day*

MARCH ⸻
Middle	Wapato, Wash.	*Indian Fair*

APRIL ⸻
Early	Warm Springs, Oreg.	*Spring Powwow*
Middle	Warm Springs, Oreg.	*Root Festival*
Late	Umatilla, Oreg.	*Umatilla Root Festival*

MAY ⸻
Early	Lapwai, Idaho	*Nez Percé Festival*
Middle	Tygh Valley, Warm Springs, Oreg.	*Tygh Celebration*
	Spokane Reservation, Wash.	*Smoo-ke-shin Powwow*
Late	Chehalis Reservation, Wash.	*Tribal Day*
Memorial Day	Swinomish Reservation, Wash.	*Festival*
	Taholah, Wash.	*Quinault days*

JUNE ⸻
Early	Colville Reservation, Wash.	*Horse event*
	Yakima Reservation, Wash.	*Games, salmon bake*
Middle	Coeur d'Alene Reservation, Idaho	*Waa-Laa days*
Late	Lummi Reservation, Wash.	*Stomish Water Carnival*
	Fort Washakie, Wyo.	*Indian days*
	La Grande, Oreg.	*Umatilla Festival*
	Craigmont, Idaho	*Nez Percé games*
	Rocky Boys Agency, Mont.	*Sun Dance*

JULY ⸻
Early	Wolf Point, Mont.	*Nez Percé games*

	Craigmont, Idaho	*Omaha dances*
	Fort Kipp, Mont.	*Indian dances*
	Warm Springs, Oreg.	*Parade, dances*
	Yakima Reservation, Wash.	*Indian Encampment*
	La Conner, Wash.	*Swinomish Festival*
	Arlee, Mont.	*Powwow*
	Colville Reservation, Wash.	*Indian Celebration*
	Taholah, Wash.	*Quinault Trout Derby*
Middle	Blackfeet Reservation, Mont.	*Indian days*
	Worley, Idaho	*Whaa-Laa Day*
	Crow Agency, Mont.	*Re-enactment of Custer's Last Stand*
	Ethete, Wyo.	*Arapaho Sun Dance*
	Browning, Mont.	*Indian days*
	Lame Deer, Mont.	*Northern Cheyenne Powwow*
Late	Ethete, Wyo.	*Arapaho Powwow*
	Poplar, Mont.	*Iron Ring Celebration*
	Fort Washakie, Wyo.	*Shoshone Sun Dance*
	Colville Reservation, Wash.	*Suds 'n' Sun Festival*
	Joseph, Oreg.	*Chief Joseph Pageant*
	Rocky Boys Agency, Mont.	*Indian days*

AUGUST ─────────────────────────────────────

Early	Kalispel Reservation, Wash.	*Powwow*
	Ashland, Mont.	*Powwow*
	Harlem, Mont.	*Powwow*
	Sheridan, Wyo.	*All-American Indian days*

	Suquamish, Wash.	*Games and clam bake*
	Fort Hall, Idaho	*Shoshone-Bannock Festival*
	Usk, Wash.	*Kalispel Powwow*
	Frazer, Mont.	*Red Bottom–Assiniboin*
Middle	Warm Springs, Oreg.	*Huckleberry Feast*
	Omak, Wash.	*Omak Stampede*
	Colville Reservation, Wash.	*Indian Fair*
	Wind River Reservation, Wyo.	*Arapaho Powwow*
	Wind River Reservation, Wyo.	*All-Indian Fair*
	Crow Agency, Mont.	*Crow Fair*
Late	Craigmont, Idaho	*Nez Percé games, feast*
	Lapwai, Idaho	*Pi-Nee-Waus days*
	Poplar, Mont.	*Oil Celebration*
	Makah Reservation, Wash.	*Dances, games*
	Thermopolis, Wyo.	*Water pageant*

_____

Labor Day . . . Weekend	Wind River, Wyo.	*Arapaho Celebration*
	Wellpinit, Wash.	*Spokane Powwow*
	Warm Springs Reservation, Oreg.	*Indian days*
	Ethete, Wyo.	*Celebration*
	Lander, Wyo.	*One-Shot Antelope Hunt*
Middle	Umatilla Reservation, Oreg.	*Pendleton Roundup*

_____

Early	Pendleton, Oreg.	*Umatilla Veterans Day*

Middle	Toppenish, Wash.	*Indian Veterans Celebration*
Late	Lapwai, Idaho	*Indian Thanksgiving*
	Umatilla Reservation, Oreg.	*Thanksgiving Potluck*

DECEMBER

Christmas . . . Week	Umatilla Reservation, Oreg.	*Indian Christmas*
	Fort Washakie, Wyo.	*Holiday dances*
	Ethete, Wyo.	*Holiday dances*
	Wind River Reservation, Wyo.	*Holiday dances*

SOUTHEAST

FEBRUARY

Late	Seminole Reservation, Hollywood, Fla.	*Seminole Powwow*

MAY

Mid-May– . . . Labor Day	Cherokee, N.C.	*Living Indian Village*

JUNE

Late June– . . Labor Day	Cherokee, N.C.	*"Unto These Hills"—Cherokee drama*

JULY

Middle	Asheville, N.C.	*Indian Craft Fair*
Late	Philadelphia, Miss.	*Choctaw Indian Fair*

OCTOBER

Early	Cherokee, N.C.	*Fall Festival*
Late	Gatlinburg, N.C.	*Indian Craft Fair*

YEAR LONG

	Seminole Reservation, Hollywood, Fla.	*Seminole Okalee Village*

NORTHEAST

JULY ─────────────────────────────

1st–Labor Day	Hogansburg, N.Y.	*Mohawk Indian Village*
Middle	Lewiston, N.Y.	*Powwow*
Late	Pleasant Point Reservation, Maine	*Indian Pageant*
	Indian Township Reservation, Maine	*Indian Pageant*
	Indian Island Reservation, Maine	*Indian Pageant*

AUGUST ─────────────────────────────

Varies	Onondaga Reservation, N.Y.	*Green Corn Dance*
	St. Regis Mohawk Reservation, N.Y.	*Green Corn Ceremony*
	Tonawanda Reservation, N.Y.	*Indian Convention*
	Tuscarora Reservation, N.Y.	*Community Fair*
Middle	Barryville, N.Y.	*Powwow*

SEPTEMBER ─────────────────────────────

Early	Southampton, N.Y.	*Powwow*

AMERICAN INDIAN MUSIC

Since most Indian records and cassettes must be ordered by mail, the names and addresses of the companies that issue them are listed below, following the identifying abbreviations used in the listings below.

ASCH: A division of Folkways; see Folk below

CAED: Caedmon Records, 1995 Broadway, New York, NY 10023.

CANY: Canyon Records, 4143 North 16th Street, Phoenix, AZ.

ELEK: Elektra Records, 665 Fifth Ave., New York, NY 10022.

FOLK: Folkways Records, 632 Broadway, New York, NY 10012.

INDIAN: Indian House, P.O. Box 472, Taos, NM 87571.

IND SHAWL: Indian Shawl, P.O. Box 47, Fay, OK 73646.

IRO: Iroqrafts, R.R. #2, Ohsweken, Ontario, Canada.

LIB CONG: Library of Congress, Music Division, Recorded Sound Section, Washington, DC 20540.

NEW WORLD: New World Records, 701 Seventh Ave., New York, NY 10036.

REQUEST: Request Records, 5937 Ravenswood Rd., Fort Lauderdale, FL 33312.

TAOS REC: Taos Recordings and Publications, P.O. Box 246, Taos, NM 87571.

COLLECTIONS

Dances and Songs, Request S-6028
American Indians of the Southwest, Folk 4420
Great Plains, Cany 6052
Healing Songs, Folk 4251
Indian Music of the Southwest, Folk 8850
Music of the Northwest Pacific, Folk 4523, two discs
North American Indian Dances, Folk 6510
Songs and Dances of the Great Lakes, Folk 4003
Sounds of Indian America, Indian 9501
War Whoops and Medicine Songs, Folk 4381
Peyote, Cany 6054
Plains Indians, Lib Cong L39
Indian Songs of Today, Lib Cong L38
Great Basin, Lib Cong L38
Northwest, Lib Cong L34
New Mexico Alabados, Taos Rec TRP-3
Pow Wow, Cany 6088
Peyote Songs, Cany 6054
Chants of the Native American Church of North America, Vols. 1, 2, and 3, Cany 6063/6068/6074
Native American Church Chants–Bright Morning Star Songs, Cany 6075
Native American Church Religious Songs, Cany 6083
Songs of Indians, Cany 6050

APACHE

Cassadore, Cany 6053
Apache Songs: Cassadore, Cany 6056
Music of Plains Apache, Asch 4252
Apache, Lib Cong L42
Philip Cassadore Sings More Apache Songs, Cany 6070
Traditional Apache Songs, Cany 6071

ARAPAHO

Social Songs of Arapaho, Cany 6080
Northern Arapaho War Dance, Ind Shawl IR 150

BLACKFEET

Blackfeet Grass Dance, Ind Shawl IR220

CHEYENNE

Great Plains Singers, Cany 6052
Plains Indians, Lib Cong L39
Northern Cheyenne War Dance, Ind Shawl IR270
Northern Cheyenne War Dance Songs, Ind Shawl IR271 and IR 303
Northern Cheyenne 49 Social Dance Songs, Ind Shawl IR 304
Southern Cheyenne War Dance, Ind Shawl IR 321
Southern Cheyenne Peyote Songs, Ind Shawl IR 321

CHIPPEWA-CREE

Twelve Chippewa War Dances, Cany 6082
Songs of the Chippewa, Lib Cong L22
Chippewa-Cree Songs, Ind Shawl IR335

COMMANCHE

Commanche Flute Music, Folk FE 4328
Commanche Peyote Songs, Vols. 1 and 2, Indian LC79-751683
Commanche-Kiowa Handgame, Indian 2501
Plains Indians, Lib Cong L39

CREEK

Songs of the Muskogee Creek, Parts 1 and 2, Indian LC 76-751693
Delaware, Cherokee, Choctaw, and Creek, Lib Cong L37

CROW

Crow Celebration, Cany 6089
Crow Grass Dance, Ind Shawl IR475
Crow War Bonnet Songs, Ind Shawl IR476

IROQUOIS

Songs from the Iroquois Longhouse, Lib Cong L6
Iroquois Social Dances, Vols. 1, 2, and 3, Iro QC 727, 728, 729

KIOWA

Kiowa 49 War Expedition Songs, Indian 2505
Kiowa Church Songs, Vol. 1, Indian 2506
Hopi and Kiowa Songs, Folk 4393
Plains Indians, Lib Cong L39
Kiowa 49 and Round Dance Songs, Cany 6087
Great Plains Singers, Cany 6052
Kiowa 49 and Round Dance, Ind Shawl IR655

NAVAJO

Memories of Navajoland-Natay, Cany 6057
Navajo Bird Tales—Junaluska, Caed S-1375
Navajo Round Dance, Indian 1504
Navajo Skip Dance and Two-Step Songs, Indian 1503

Navajo Songs, Cany 6055
Navajo Sway Songs, Indian 1501
Sioux and Navajo, Folk 4401
Night and Daylight Yeibichei, Indian 1502
Navajo, Lib Cong L41
Natay, Navajo Singer, Cany 6160
Traditional Navajo Song, Cany 6064
Navajo Squaw Dance Songs, Cany 6067
Yei-Chai Chants, Cany 6069
Navajo Social Songs, Cany 6076
My Beautiful Land, Cany 6078
Navajo Gift Songs, Indian IH 1505

PAPAGO

Songs of the Papago, Lib Cong L31
Traditional Papago Music, Vol. 1, Cany 6084
Chicken Scratch and Popular Music, Cany 6085

PAWNEE

Pawnees Music–Evarts, Folk 4334
Songs of the Pawnee and North Ute, Lib Cong L25

PONCA

Ponca War Dance, Vols. 1 and 2, Indian LC R68-471
Ponca Peyote Songs, Vols. 1 and 2, Indian IH 2005/2006

PUEBLO

Taos Pueblo Round Dance, two discs, Indian LC 78-751680
Taos Round Dance, Vols. 1 and 2, Indian LC-R68-478
Zuñi-Questawki and Shebaba Groups, Cany 6060
Pueblo Indians, Lib Cong L43
San Juan Songs, Cany 6065
Summer Songs from Zuñi, Cany 6077
Ditch-Cleaning and Picnic Songs of Picuris Pueblo, Indian IH 1051
Taos Indian Songs, Taos Rec TRP-1
Picuris Songs, Taos Rec IRP-5
More Taos Songs, Taos Rec IRP-7
Picuris Pueblo "So These Won't Be Forgotten . . . ," Taos Rec TRP-121
Taos Spanish Songs, Taos Rec TRP-2
"Buenos Dias, Paloma Blance," Taos Rec TRP-122
Taos Matachines Music, Taos Rec TRP-4
Bailes de Taos, Taos Rec TRP-6

Hopi-Katchina, Folk 4394
Hopi-Kiowa, Folk 4393
Hopi Butterfly, Cany 6072

SIOUX

Crow Dog's Paradise: Songs of the Sioux, Elek 74091
Sioux and Navajo, Folk 4401
Sioux Favorites, Cany 6059
Songs of the Sioux: Rosebud Reservation, Cany 6062
Fort Kipp Sioux Singers, Cany 6079
William Horncloud Sings Sioux Rabbit Songs, Cany 6081
Sioux Grass Songs, Cany 6086
Sioux Fast War Dance Songs, Ind Shawl IR1193
Sioux Grass Dance Songs, Ind Shawl IR 1194
Sioux Songs, Ind Shawl IR1191
Sioux, Lib Cong L40
Bear Singers of Tama, Iowa, with War Dance Songs, Cany 6090
Sioux Fort Peck Popular Juniors, Ind Shawl IR1190

MISCELLANEOUS TRIBES

Shoshone: War Dance, Ind Shawl IR1165
Great Basin, Lib Cong L38
Laguna, Cany 6058
Arickara, Ind Shawl IR175
Gros Ventre and Assiniboine, Ind Shawl IR490
Omaha, Ind Shawl IR825
Winnebago, Ind Shawl IR 1310
Umatilla, Ind Shawl IR 1280
Songs of Earth, Water, Fire, and Sky, New World 246
Songs of Love, Luck, Animals, and Magic, New World 297
Songs of the Pima, Cany 6066
Songs of the Nootka and Quileute, Lib Cong L32
Songs of the Yuma, Cocopa and Yaqui, Lib Cong L24
Seneca Songs from Coldspring Longhouse, Lib Cong L17
Songs of the Menominee, Mandan and Hidatsa, Lib Cong L33
Mandan and Hidatsa Grass Dance Songs, Ind Shawl IR740
Flathead Indian Music, Folk 4445
Mushroom Ceremony of the Mazatec Indians of Mexico, Folk 8975

BIBLIOGRAPHY

Alexander, H. B. *Mystery of Life*, Open Court, 1913.

Bahti, Tom. *Southwestern Indian Ceremonials*, KC Publications, 1947.

Barrett, S. A. *Ceremonies of the Pomo Indians*, University of California Press, 1914.

Basso, Keith H. *The Cibecue Apache*, Holt, Rinehart & Winston, 1970.

Bierhorst, John. *Four Classics of Indian Literature*, Farrar, Straus, & Giroux, 1974.

Brown, Joseph E. *The North American Indians, A Selection of Photographs by Edward S. Curtis*, Aperture, 1972.

Bunzel, Ruth L. *Zuñi Katchinas*, Bureau of American Ethnology, Annual Report 47, 1929–30.

Buttree, Julia M. *The Rhythm of the Redman*, Barnes, 1930.

Campbell, Joseph. *The Hero with a Thousand Faces*, Princeton, 1973.

————. *The Way of the Animal Powers, Vol. 1*, Van der Marck, 1983.

Chafe, Wallace L. *Seneca Thanksgiving Rituals*, Bureau of American Ethnology, No. 19, 1961.

Curtis, Edward S. *North American Indian, 1907*. Reprint, A. & W. Visual Library, 1975.

Densmore, Frances. *Chippewa Music, Parts 1 and 2*, Bureau of American Ethnology, Bulletin 58, 1929.

————. *Teton Sioux Music*, Bureau of American Ethnology, 1918.

————. *Menominee Music*, Bureau of American Ethnology, 1932.

————. *Nootka and Quileute Music*, Bureau of American Ethnology, 1939.

————. *Pawnee Music*, Bureau of American Ethnology, 1929.

————. *Seminole Music*, Bureau of American Ethnology, 1956.

————. *Yuman and Yaqui Music*, Bureau of American Ethnology, 1932.

Dorsey, George A. *The Cheyenne: The Sun Dance*, Chicago Field Museum, 1905.

Dutton, Bertha P. *Sun Father's Way: The Kiva Murals of Kuana*, University of New Mexico Press, 1963.

Evans, May G., and Evans, Bessie. *American Indian Dance Steps*, Barnes, 1931.

Fenton, William N. *An Outline of Seneca Ceremonies at Coldspring Longhouse*, Yale University Publications in Anthropology, No. 9, 1936.

Fewkes, J. Walter. *Hopi Katchinas*, Bureau of American Ethnology, 1903 (Rio Grande Press, 1969).

————. *The Snake Ceremonials at Walpi*, Houghton Mifflin, 1894.

La Flesche, Francis. *War Ceremony and Peace Ceremony of the Osage Indians*, Bureau of American Ethnology, 1939.

Fletcher, Alice C. *The Hako: A Pawnee Ceremony, Part 2*, Bureau of American Ethnology, 1900–1901.

Goddard, Pliny E. *Dancing Societies of the Sarsi Indians*, American Museum of Natural History, 1914.

Hewitt, J. N. B. *Iroquoian Cosmology, Parts 1 and 2*, Bureau of American Ethnology, 1899–1900; 1925–1926.

Highwater, Jamake. *Dance: Rituals of Experience*, A&W, 1978.

————. *Fodor's Indian America: A Cultural and Travel Guide*, David McKay, 1975.

————. *Song From the Earth, American Indian Painting*, New York Graphic Society (Little, Brown), 1976.

Javitch, Gregory; *Selective Bibliography of Ceremonies, Dance, Music and Song of American Indians*, Osiris, Montreal, 1974.

Josephy, Alvin, Jr. *The Indian Heritage of America*, Alfred A. Knopf, 1968.

Kurath, Gertrude P. *Iroquois Music and Dance*, Bureau of American Ethnology, No. 187, 1964.

Laski, Vera. *Seeking Life, The Raingod Ceremony of San Juan*, American Folklore Society, 1958.

Linton, Ralph. *Annual Ceremony of the Pawnee Medicine Men*, Chicago Field Museum, 1922.

————. *The Sacrifice to the Morning Star by the Skidi Pawnee*, Chicago Field Museum, 1922.

Lowie, Robert H. *Sun Dance of the Shoshone, Ute and Hidatsa*, American Museum of Natural History, 1919.

Marriott, Alice, and Rachlin, Carol K. *Peyote*. Thomas Y. Crowell, 1971.

Matthews, Washington. *The Mountain Chant*, Bureau of American Ethnology, 1887.

————. *Navajo Legends*, American Folklore Society, 1897.

————. *The Night Chant, Memoirs, Vol. 6*, American Museum of Natural History, May, 1902

Merriam, C. H. *Studies of California Indians*, University of California Press, 1962.

Mooney, James. *The Ghost Dance Religion*, Bureau of American Ethnology, 1892–1893.

Ortiz, Alfonso. *The Tewa World*, University of Chicago Press, 1969.

Painter, Muriel Thayer. *A Yaqui Easter*, University of Arizona Press, 1971.

Parsons, Elsie Clews. *The Pueblo of Jemez*, Phillips Academy, 1925.

————. *Pueblo Indian Religion, Vols. 1 and 2*, University of Chicago, 1939.

————. *The Scalp Ceremonial of Zuñi*, American Anthropological Association, 1928.

Radin, Paul. *The Road of Life and Death*, Bollingen Series V, 1945.

Reed, Verner Z. "The Ute Bear Dance," *American Anthropology*, vol. 9, July 1896.

Russell, Frank. *The Pima Indians*, Bureau of American Ethnology, 1908.

Smithsonian Institution, *The Year of the Hopi, Paintings and Photographs by Joseph Mora, 1904–06*, 1979.

Speck, Frank G., and Broom, Leonard. *Cherokee Dance and Drama*, University of California Press, 1951.

Spicer, Edward H., and Balastrero, Phyllis. "Yaqui Easter Ceremonial," *Arizona Highways*, vol. 47, no. 3, March 1971.

Stephen, Alexander M. *Hopi Journal, Vols. 1 and 2*, Columbia University Contributions to Anthropology, vol. 23, 1936.

Stevenson, Matilda C. *The Sia*, Bureau of American Ethnology, 1894.

———. *The Zuñi Indians*, Bureau of American Ethnology, 1904.

Tedlock, Dennis, and Tedlock, Barbara (eds.). *Teachings from the American Earth: Indian Religion and Philosophy*, Liveright, 1975.

Tooker, Elizabeth. *Iroquois Ceremonial of Midwinter*, Syracuse University Press, 1970.

Underhill, Ruth M. *Singing for Power*, University of California Press, 1938.

———. *Red Man's Religion*, University of Chicago Press, 1965.

Waters, Frank, *The Book of the Hopi*, Viking, 1963.

Webb, William, and Weinstein, Robert A. *Dwellers at the Source, Southwestern Indian Photographs by A.C. Vroman, 1895-1904*, Grossman/Viking, 1973.

White, Leslie A. *The Acoma Indians*, Bureau of American Ethnology, Annual Report 27, 1929–1930.

Whitman, William III. "The Pueblo Indians of San Ildefonso," Columbia University Contributions to Anthropology, vol. 34, 1947.

Wilder, Carleton, S. *The Yaqui Deer Dance*, Bureau of American Ethnology, No. 66, 1963.

Witthoft, John. *Green Corn Ceremonialism in the Eastern Woodlands*, Contributions from the Museum of Anthropology of the University of Michigan, No. 13, 1949.

Wright, Barton. *Kachinas, A Hopi Indian's Documentary*, Northland Press, 1973.

Yazzie, Ethelous (ed.). *Navajo History, Vol. 1*, Navajo Community College Press, 1971.

PHOTO CREDITS

American Museum of Natural History, New York: 46–47, 75, 159.

Arizona State Museum, University of Arizona, Tucson: 27 *(Simeon Schwemberger)*; 30; 64–65 *(F. Hanna)*; 71, 145 *(C. M. Wood)*.

British Columbia Provincial Museum, Victoria: 151.

Bureau of Indian Affairs, Washington, D.C.: 142.

Denver Public Library (Western History Department), Denver: 12–13; 100 center *(A. C. Vroman)*; 104–105 top; 125; 146.

Farrar, Strauss & Giroux, New York: 45 *(J. Bierhorst)*.

Humboldt State University (Humboldt County Collection), California: 18–19, 123 *(A. W. Ericson)*.

Jamake Highwater Collection, New York: 72, 143 top.

John R. Wilson Collection, Tulsa, Oklahoma: 86, 87, 93, 102, 103, 106 *(Jacinto Mora)*.

Mennonite Library and Archives, North Newton, Kansas: 84 bottom; 85; 94 top; 95; 96 left; 101 bottom *(H. R. Voth)*; 104 bottom.

Museum of New Mexico, Santa Fe: 100 top *(Ben Wittick)*; 100 bottom *(H. F. Robinson)*; 124 *(Ben Wittick)*.

Museum of the American Indian, New York: 49, 70, 82, 155, 160.

National Collection of Fine Arts, Washington, D.C.: 56–57 *(George Catlin)*.

Natural History Museum of Los Angeles County (History Division), Los Angeles: 78; 94 bottom; 97; 98–99; 101 top; 110–111 *(A. C. Vroman)*.

New Mexico Department of Development, Santa Fe: 69 bottom, 109, 143 right, 148–149.

Oklahoma Department of Recreation, Oklahoma City: 143 left; 144 top, 147 *(Fred W. Marvel)*.

Oklahoma Historical Society, Oklahoma City: 2–3.

Philadelphia Museum of Art: 16–17; 20–21; 22; 51; 58; 88–89; 120, 165, 169 *(Edward S. Curtis)*.

Provincial Archives, Victoria, B.C.: 158.

Smithsonian Institution (National Anthropological Archives), Washington, D.C.: 6–7 *(Frances Densmore)*; 10–11 *(Matilda Coxe Stevenson)*; 24–25 *(James Mooney)*; 31 *(A. F. Randall)*; 52–53 *(Matilda Coxe Stevenson)*; 74 *(Sumner W. Matteson)*; 76 *(Matilda Coxe Stevenson)*; 90–91 *(James Mooney)*; 121; 157; 167 *(Sumner W. Matteson)*.

South Dakota Department of Highways (Travel Division), Pierre: 14.

University of Oklahoma Library (Western History Collection), Norman 34–35 *(W. E. Hollon)*; 55 *(Alice Marriott)*; 136, 162–163 *(The Shuck Collection)*.

Western Ways Features, Tucson: 44, 60, 61, 62, 63, 66, 67, 69 bottom, 126, 127, 128, 129, 130, 131, 137, 139 *(Charles Herbert)*.

INDEX

ramada, 139

rattles, *11*, *52*, *74*, *75*, 108, *122*, 127, *149*

Red Ute, 59

Redheaded Woodpecker Dance, *122–123*

reed grass, 40

religion, 119–125

rhythm, 30

ribbons, 63, 130

Rio Grande Pueblos, *72*, 100, 105

Rivera, Diego, 122

roach, hair, *12*, 153

Road of Life, 83

rodeo, *143*

rosary, 127

roundhouse, 139

running water, 135

rushes, *50*

Sachs, Curt, 140

Sacred Dance, 152

Sacred Lake, *111*

saguaro fruit, 139

Saguaro National Monument, 137

Salish, *22*

San Ildefonso Pueblo, New Mexico, 55

San Juan Pueblo, New Mexico, 68, 108–118

San Xavier, Arizona, *145*

Sanctifying Rite, 114

sand paintings, 39, 44, *45*, 100

Santa Clara Pueblo, New Mexico, *11*, *149*

Sayatasha, *124*

Scalp Dance, 105

scalps, 153

scratching, *6*

Season Dance, *145*

Second Earth, 154

secrecy, 23

self-mutilation, 152–153

self-torture, 152–153, *158*

Seminoles, 6–7

sexuality, 77, 82

  see also obscenity

shade house, *see* kisi

Shalako Ceremony, *124–125*

shaman, 49–50, 52–53, 60–67, *76*

Shoshone, 49, 121, *142*

Shungopovi, 94

silence, 32

Silent One, 117–118

Sioux, 58–59, 152

sipapuni, 99, 100

Sitting Bull, 161

Skipping Dance, *145*

skull, buffalo, 155

skunk, *11*

Slayer of the Alien Powers, *46*

Slim First Dancers, *46*

Smith, Edward D. and Virginia W., 36

Snake Dance, 95, 100–101

snakes, 100–101

Sokoyo, *91*

Soldiers of the Virgin, 127

solitude, 32

Son (in Pawnee Hako Ceremony), 132–135

songs, 32, 119

Songs of the Whirling Logs, 45

South Dakota, 161

Southern Plains Handgame, 142

Soyal, *86*

Spider Woman, 100

spiritual body, 28, 166, 168

sport, *144*

Spotted Eagle, *156–157*

spruce, 41, 61, 108, *111*

Squaw Dance, *146*

Stick Game, *142*

stomp step, 141

Stone Man Lake, 114

Stone Man Mountain, 114

sumac, 39

Summer People, 108

sun, 160

Sun, Chant to the, 134

Sun Dance, 2–3, 145, 152–159

Sun Dance Lodge, 154

Sun Lodge, 153

Sun Rain Power, 116

sun shield, 99

Suns, 119

sweathouse, 40, 42, 44, 63

Sweet Meats, 117–118

Tablita Dance, *10–11*

tablitas, *11*, 94, 103

Talking Power, 27, *34–35*, 39, 40–43, *46*, 72

tall tales, 9

tawitshpa, 132

Tcirkwena Dance, *145*

technology, 168

temples, 119

tepees, 61, 154

Tesuque Pueblo, *143*

Teton Dakota, 119

Tewa, *10–11*, 108–118

theocracy, 119

Third Earth, 155

Third Rain Power, 116

thunder, 112, 115

Thunder Being, 73

Thunder Lake, 114

Thunder Songs, 44

Thunderbird, 48, *121*

Thunderbird's Nest, *2–3*, 156

Tira'wa, 131–133, 135, 136

tobacco, 40, 133

Tobadshistshini, 41, 46

toe-heel step, 141

Toharu, 135

torture, self-, 152–153, *158*

Turquoise People, 108

turtle shell, *11*, *75*, 108

Two Boys, *74*

Two-Horned Priests, 84, 85

underground chambers, *see* kivas

understatement, 33

Utah, 36

Utes, 37, 59

victory dance, *12*, 105

Virgin, soldiers of the, 127

virgin girls, 109

visions, 24, 79, 133–134

voice production, 29

vomiting, 101

wakanda, *121*

Waking Song, 43

Walpi Pueblo, Arizona, 121

wands, 40, 62, 67, 127

War Dance, *12–13*, 144, 153

Warriors' Tepee, 154

Watacka Naamu, *91*

water, 112, 135

Waters, Frank, 83

Weitchpee, California, *122*

whips, 108, 115, *149*

whistles, *74*, *156*, 158

White Deer Dance, *122*

White Deerskin Dance, *18–19*

White-Faced Kachina Girl, *93*

White-Painted Woman, 60

Wild Turkey Woman, *55*, *88*

wildcat, 131

Wilson, Jack, 160

wind, 28, 29, 115

Window Rock, 26

wine, 139

Winter Dance, *16–17*

Winter Men, 110–118

Winter People, 108

Winter Rain Dance, *145*